HOW TO GET
INTO
U.S. SERVICE ACADEMIES

HOW TO GET INTO U.S. SERVICE ACADEMIES

by
William Bennett Cassidy
Foreword by Colonel Pierce A. Rushton, Jr., Director
of Admissions, U.S. Military Academy, West Point

An Arco Book
Published by Prentice Hall Press
New York, New York 10023

An Arco Book
Published by Prentice Hall Press
A Division of Simon & Schuster, Inc.
Gulf+Western Building
One Gulf+Western Plaza
New York, New York 10023

PRENTICE HALL PRESS is a trademark of Simon & Schuster, Inc.

Manufactured in the United States of America
1 2 3 4 5 6 7 8 9 10

Library of Congress Cataloging-in-Publication Data

Cassidy, William.
    How to get into U.S. service academies.

    ''An Arco book.''
    Bibliography: p.
    1. Military education—United States. I. Title.
U408.C37   1986   355′.007′1173   86-22557
ISBN 0-668-06596-6

CONTENTS

PART TWO: SAMPLE ENTRANCE EXAMINATIONS

FOREWORD

Because you are interested in a service academy as a possible college choice for yourself or someone you know, you have probably also formed an image of it. That image most likely includes rousing football games, parades, and graduations but is also somewhat mysterious! Certainly, you must learn about other aspects of the service academies before making a commitment to attend one of them.

The United States service academies are an integral part of our nation's national defense. They provide the thousands of young men and women who enter each year with a unique opportunity to obtain a quality education leading to varied, significant careers in the armed forces. The academic flexibility currently available to the service academy student has evolved to meet the needs of both the nation and the individual. The nation gains trained, educated young officers who have the necessary character and intellectual foundation for their positions.

Like many students attending competitive colleges, new cadets cite the academic program as their primary reason for choosing the service academies. These academies, however, are much more than just four-year undergraduate programs. They provide future officers with their first professional military experience. They also offer an extraordinary opportunity for personal development and the acquisition of leadership and management skills crucial in military service.

A cadet's or midshipman's experience at a service academy is far from a "picnic in uniform." Like any worthwhile pursuit, it requires many personal sacrifices. It is physically and emotionally challenging, as it must be to produce officers able to make decisions in stressful situations and at the same time earn the respect of those they command and the country they serve.

Discipline is a key word at the service academies. To be prepared for commissioned service you must expect demands on your time, a certain degree of pressure, and some limitations on personal freedom. Their daily regimen is designed to develop in cadets an appreciation of the highest professional standards. The student quickly learns to take that extra effort, budget his or her time wisely, and establish a clear set of priorities.

The service academies are among the last institutions of higher learning that continue to observe and enforce an honor code as an integral part of the student's collegiate experience. The honor system promotes integrity as a matter of course—a fundamental prerequisite for service to country as an officer.

The motive of "service to country" is increasingly evident among today's applicants. The West Point motto of *Duty, honor, country* symbolizes the service academies' commitment to proper values, integrity, and dedication within the military profession.

All of us responsible for service academy admissions programs are delighted with the quality and interest of our candidates. The admissions message to all outstanding young men and women contemplating the service academy as a college choice is to take a good look at all of them. The best approach is to start an admissions file at the end of the junior year in high school. Read about the academies, discuss and visit them— motivate yourself to learn all you can about them. Discuss the opportunities and challenges with graduates and cadets. You will then be able to make an informed decision whether to pursue your application. Accept an offer of admission only if the academy's program corresponds to your own abilities and aspirations and, of course, if you have a strong desire to tackle military service.

The service academies are indeed special places. One of them may be for you or someone you know. Take the time to find out!

PIERCE A. RUSHTON, JR.
Colonel, U.S. Army
Director of Admissions
U.S. Military Academy

INTRODUCTION
TRAINING TOMORROW'S LEADERS

Leaving secondary school is an exciting, but sometimes frightening, step toward maturity. After high school you alone are responsible for your actions. You must make the decisions that will shape your career.

Many students begin considering, if not actively planning, their careers long before they graduate. Parents, teachers, guidance counselors, peers, and most important, personal judgment lead them to a particular choice—whether to attend college, opt for advanced vocational training, or begin working.

Today, more and more young men and women are looking seriously at the career opportunities offered by the military. Their reasons range from patriotism to the attractions of job security and high-level training offered by the five academies. The professionalism fostered by these institutions, and the experience gained as a commissioned officer, are valuable assets coveted by both the military and the civilian world.

Each academy offers its students unique opportunities both to serve their country and to advance themselves professionally. Before students can benefit from those opportunities, however, they must make a firm commitment to a particular service. Entering a service academy normally means serving in the armed forces for several years after graduation.

It is therefore important that you know exactly what your prospective academy has to offer. This book helps by providing an introduction to each academy.

In addition to skill and knowledge, the most important ingredient in any successful career is motivation. One naval academy midshipman, when asked by the academy's superintendent to advise potential students, replied: "Don't come here for the prestige . . . or for the free education. And don't come if you are pushed by parents, or friends, or relatives." If you decide to enter a service academy, the decision must be your own.

Part One

An In-Depth Look
At The Five Academies

1

THE U.S. MILITARY ACADEMY AT WEST POINT

Background Information

The United States Military Academy (USMA) at West Point, New York, is the oldest of the five service academies. West Point has been training and educating young men for careers as professional Regular Army officers since 1802. Women have attended the academy since 1976, after federal legislation in 1975 enabled them to enter and participate fully in the programs offered by all service academies.

West Point is situated 50 miles north of New York City at a strategic bend in the Hudson River. The Point was an important link in the nation's chain of defenses during the American Revolution—if the British had gained control of the Hudson Valley they would have divided the colonies. George Washington had the Point fortified in 1778 to prevent a British advance from New York or Canada, making West Point the oldest continually occupied military facility in the country. The academy today covers approximately sixteen thousand acres, most of which are used for military exercises and training.

United States Corps of Cadets

When you enroll in the academy you automatically join the Corps of Cadets, a unit of the United States Army. You must therefore agree to accept special obligations and restrictions. For example, as a cadet you must agree to serve in the Army for at least five years after graduating from the academy. Also, you may not marry before leaving the academy. However, cadets are entitled to Army benefits.

The Corps of Cadets forms a brigade divided into four regiments, each with three battalions. Upperclassmen lead the corps and receive leadership counseling from academy officials. In turn, the upperclassmen counsel and guide new cadets. Each cadet's ability to lead others is regularly assessed and rated.

Cadets earn their leave (vacations) and free time through advancement and superior performance. Upperclassmen have more free time than new cadets, and first class cadets (seniors) receive more weekend passes than second class cadets (juniors). Fourth class cadets, or plebes, are granted little free time, since their first year is considered crucial to their academic and professional development. Other than the holiday leave they receive during the Christmas season, fourth class cadets are allowed only four weekends away from the academy. All cadets receive some summer leave, and upperclassmen are granted spring leave. Cadets who exhibit special merit in individual or unit performance may be given extra weekend passes.

Cadets are also paid a regular salary. Each cadet earns over $6,500 a year, part of

The West Point plaque expresses the values of honor and commitment that have been associated with the academy since its founding. (U.S. Army Photograph)

which is expected to cover uniforms and textbooks. Medical and dental care is free for all academy students, and personal and legal counseling is also readily available.

Dormitories, called barracks at West Point, are clustered around Washington Hall, which contains the Corps of Cadets' headquarters and dining facilities. Some classrooms and laboratories are also located in Washington Hall. Thayer, Bartlett, and Mahan halls hold the remainder. The 500,000-volume cadet library is nearby.

Other campus facilities include a cadet activities center with an auditorium, restaurant, and ballroom; three chapels where Catholic, Jewish, and Protestant services are held; a gymnasium with five separate gym areas, four swimming pools, and various rooms reserved for squash, handball, weight training, and combative sports; indoor rifle and pistol ranges; a hockey rink; and a variety of outdoor athletic facilities, including a track, baseball diamond, and football stadium.

West Point's lifestyle is carefully structured to develop integrity, discipline, and a sense of duty in each cadet. This is accomplished through academic, physical, and military training and enforcement of the academy's honor code: *A cadet will not lie,*

West Point, located in the historic Hudson River Valley north of New York City, is the oldest continually occupied military facility in this country. (U.S. Army Photograph)

cheat, or steal, nor tolerate those who do. Significantly, the honor code was created and is enforced by the Corps of Cadets, not the academy's administrators.

Most military training is held in the summer, when cadets participate in field exercises or serve with active Army units, sometimes overseas. Cadets must complete West Point's military science and physical education programs as well as 44 semester-long courses to earn a Bachelor of Science degree from the academy.

Academic Life

Though the academy was founded to provide the nation with qualified military engineers—the engineers who designed most of nineteenth-century America's infrastructure—its current curriculum provides cadets with a broad collegiate and military education. In addition to the 32-course core program required of all cadets, West Point offers several fields of study as well as optional majors to those who wish to intensify their study of a particular academic area.

The curriculum is divided into two tracks, mathematics–science–engineering and

Cadets passing in review. (U.S. Army Photograph)

humanities–public affairs. Cadets choose a track at the end of their plebe year and either a major or field of study at the end of their third class (sophomore) year. The MSE track offers 10 fields of study and eight majors; the HPA track offers 17 fields of study and eight majors. For the optional majors cadets are required to complete a senior research project or thesis.

The academy's academic program is designed to produce the creative and resourceful officers sought by today's Army. To do so, its academic staff must keep up with the latest national and international trends and standards in their fields.

Classes are small, ranging typically from 12 to 16 students, to ensure that cadets get individual attention. Classes are arranged according to student ability, and so those who need to concentrate on certain fundamental subjects may do so while those who are better prepared may move ahead more quickly. A reading improvement program and courses in computer literacy are available to those who wish to get a better grasp of the basics.

The USMA library, one of the foremost institutions of its kind in the nation, is a boon to both cadets and researchers. It holds 500,000 volumes, 8,600 records, television cassettes, and educational tapes, and receives about 2,000 newspapers and periodicals from American and foreign publishers. It maintains its reputation as one of the best technical libraries in the United States. The library is currently expanding its computer system, which automates circulation and makes items easier to find.

The academy is committed to the use of computers in undergraduate education. More than 200 remote terminals installed throughout the campus allow students access to the academy's computer system for direct instruction in a variety of computer applica-

The dining facilities at West Point. (U.S. Army Photograph)

tions. Microcomputers are also used by individual departments to supplement classroom instruction.

West Point sponsors a vigorous lecture series that brings recognized authorities in various fields to its campus. Among the speakers who have visited the academy recently are George Will, the political columnist; Carl Sagan, astronomer, author, and television narrator; Isaac Singer, Nobel Laureate; Barbara Tuchman, historian and author; and Fred Friendly, former president of CBS News.

Military Training

Military education is provided by the Office of the Commandant, United States Corps of Cadets. The departments of military instruction and physical education handle most of the cadets' military training.

Plebes start their first year at West Point during the summer with a six-week basic training program in the fundamental skills of soldiering. It is the beginning of a year-long, rigorous indoctrination in military practices. Discipline, confidence, and duty are stressed throughout the program; a regimen of physical exercise gets plebes into

There are three separate chapels at West Point for Catholic, Protestant, and Jewish services.
(U.S. Army Photograph)

Cadets listening to instructions for firing an artillery piece. (U.S. Army Photograph)

"combat shape." By living as Army recruits, academy officials point out, cadets are better able to understand and respect the enlisted men they will someday command. Military instruction during the academic year is centered on the American military heritage, professional behavior, small unit tactics, and map reading.

In the summer of their sophomore year, cadets receive military field training—an extended period of artillery firing, field communications, infantry operations, military engineering, mountaineering, and survival courses. They spend most of that time at Camp Buckner, based at West Point, and one week at Fort Knox, Kentucky, where they are given the basics of tank, cavalry, mechanized infantry, self-propelled field artillery, and air-defense operations. During the fall semester they study combined arms operations, company/team task force operations, and terrain analysis, with an emphasis on the use of satellite imagery and photographic interpretation.

For their second class (junior) summer, cadets are offered a choice of training in Panamanian jungles or the Alaskan tundra. They are also offered training courses in parachuting (airborne training), helicopter pilot training, scuba training through the Naval Special Warfare Course, or survival training in the rugged land surrounding the Air Force academy in Colorado.

That training is followed by cadet troop leader training, which permits cadets to fill junior officer positions in active Army units, or the drill cadet program, which stations cadets at basic training facilities as noncommissioned officers assigned to instruct trainees. Further military training during the second class year focuses on Army maintenance, personnel, supply, and training systems.

In their first class summer, senior cadets lead third and fourth class cadets in the military exercises at Camp Bruckner and basic training. They then take leadership positions in the Corps of Cadets and concentrate on planning, organizing, and directing its activities.

Academic training at the academy is rigorous and standards are high. Pictured is a cadet in the chemistry lab. (U.S. Army Photograph)

"Every Cadet an Athlete"

West Point places special emphasis on physical conditioning. Each cadet is expected to be physically prepared for duty as an officer. Participation in sports programs at the intramural, club, or collegiate levels—as well as completion of West Point's four-year physical education program—prepares cadets to meet, and often exceed, the academy's expectations.

Although football is perhaps the most popular of the academy's sports programs, it is only one part of the varied intercollegiate athletic program offered by West Point. Other sports include baseball, basketball, golf, hockey, lacrosse, marksmanship, soccer, squash, swimming, tennis, indoor and outdoor track, water polo, and wrestling.

Female cadets compete as actively as their male counterparts. The women's cross country and track teams have built an impressive record of victories since their integration into the academy's sports program. Women also compete in intercollegiate softball, tennis, and volleyball.

The academy offers club and intramural sports to those cadets not active at the official intercollegiate level. Clubs are divided into two categories, athletic and recreational, and their teams compete against clubs from other colleges and universities. Cycling, fencing, women's gymnastics, lacrosse, marathon, orienteering, rugby, sail-

Cadets in the physics lab. (U.S. Army Photograph)

ing, skiing, women's soccer, sport parachute, team handball, triathlon, men's volley-ball, and freestyle wrestling are all club sports included in the athletic category. The recreational club sports offered are bowling, handball, judo, karate, powerlifting, rac-quetball, riding, and skeet and trap shooting. Many club teams also earn intercolle-giate honors.

In addition to intercollegiate or club sports, each cadet competes semiweekly in the intramural sports program. Participation is voluntary during the spring. Among the in-tramural sports at West Point are flickerball, football, soccer, triathlon, track, basket-ball, boxing, handball, squash, swimming, volleyball, and wrestling. Lacrosse, cross country, tennis, and softball are added to the list in the spring.

How to Apply for Admission

To be accepted into the USMA you must meet the requirements of public law as well as the academy's academic, physical, and mental standards. Admissions officers judge each candidate on the basis of his or her academic and medical records, physical con-dition, and leadership potential.

To apply for admission: (1) Determine whether you meet West Point's require-ments; (2) apply for a nomination; (3) start a file at West Point; (4) fill out the forms

The physical education program is competitive and varied, for the academy places a strong emphasis on physical conditioning. Pictured are cadets working out. (U.S. Army Photograph)

supplied by the military academy admissions office and Department of Defense medical examination review board; (5) take the Scholastic Aptitude Test (SAT) or the American College Testing Assessment Program Exam (ACT); (6) take the academy's qualifying medical exam; and (7) take the academy's physical aptitude exam.

To enter West Point you must:

- be at least 17 but not yet 22 years old by July 1 of the year you plan to enter the academy
- be an American citizen at the time of enrollment (however, foreign students nominated with the agreement of the United States and their native country may enroll)
- be "trustworthy, emotionally stable, and motivated" based on interviews and recommendations
- be single
- not be pregnant
- have no legal obligation to support a child (this stipulation, of course, applies to men and women)

- have a superior academic record
- perform well on the SAT or ACT
- be in general good health and pass the academy's medical exam
- have superior strength, endurance, and agility
- pass the academy's physical exam

West Point encourages you to pursue a college-preparatory course in high school. Your high school curriculum should include four years of English and mathematics, two years of foreign language and laboratory science experience, and a year of chemistry, physics, and American history. Students are also urged to take elective courses in government, geography, and economics.

USMA Preparatory School

Some students may want to attend the academy's preparatory school. The school offers a comprehensive 10-month review of high school English and mathematics while providing an introduction to college-level composition and to military life.

Students apply to the preparatory school as they would to the academy and must compete with other applicants for nomination to West Point after graduating.

The preparatory school's curriculum includes literature, grammar, algebra, geometry and solid geometry, trigonometry and spherical trigonometry, and calculus. A computer-math elective is offered also.

Applying for a Nomination

You should apply for a nomination to West Point in the spring of your high school junior year. The sample letter on page 12 serves as a guide to the proper nomination request.

You must also fill out the precandidate questionnaire available from the academy. A file is established for you by the academy's admissions office when they have received the completed form. Other required USMA and Department of Defense medical forms are added to the file as they are received by the admissions office.

The officials authorized to nominate candidates for cadetships are:

- **the Vice President**, who may nominate five candidates annually from anywhere in the United States;
- **members of Congress**, who may nominate five candidates per year; senators nominate candidates from their states and representatives nominate candidates from their congressional districts;
- **congressional delegates** from the District of Columbia (five nominations per year), the Virgin Islands (two nominations each year), and Guam (two nominations each year); delegates from Guam and the Virgin Islands may nominate candidates from their respective islands only;
- **the governor and resident commissioner of Puerto Rico**, who together may nominate six candidates per year—the governor, a native Puerto Rican and the resident commissioner, five residents of Puerto Rico;
- **the governor of American Samoa**, who may nominate one Samoan candidate annually.

*This format is intended as a guide. A separate letter must be sent
to each Senator and Representative to whom you apply.*

FORMAT

REQUEST FOR CONGRESSIONAL NOMINATION

Date _____

The Honorable _____   The Honorable _____
United States Senate   House of Representatives
Washington, D.C. 20510   OR   Washington, D.C. 20515

Dear Senator _____   Dear Mr./Ms. _____

    I desire to attend the United States Military Academy and to be commissioned in the Regular Army. I respectfully request that I be considered as one of your nominees for the class entering West Point in July 1985.

    The following data are furnished for your information:

Name: _____

Permanent Address: _____

Telephone Number: _____

Temporary Address and telephone number (if different from preceding):

_____

_____

Date of Birth: _____

High School: _____

Social Security Number: _____

Names of Parents: _____

    I have/have not requested that a precandidate file by initiated for me at the West Point Admissions Office.

Sincerely,

When a member of Congress submits a list of nominees to the Department of the Army, he or she indicates how they should be evaluated. The department may judge the nominees as "congressional competitors," ranking the candidates according to their qualifications, or a candidate may be selected as the principal nominee, with alternates being nominated only if the principal is rejected. If the principal is not qualified for admission, each alternate is evaluated in the order chosen by the nominator.

In addition to these officials, the Secretary of the Army is qualified to allocate cadetships including 100 presidential nominations, 85 nominations for enlisted members of the Army Reserve or National Guard, 20 nominations for students enrolled in honor military and naval schools or ROTC programs, and an unlimited number of nominations to the sons and daughters of persons awarded the Congressional Medal of Honor.

Qualifying for an Army Nomination

Presidential nominations may be granted only to the sons and daughters of career personnel from any branch of the military. Children of reservists who did not retire on active duty, however, are ineligible. Enlisted members of the Regular Army, Army Reserve, and Army National Guard must make sure they are in compliance with the Army's AR 351-12 regulations when applying for an academy nomination.

If you are the son or daughter of a deceased or 100 percent disabled veteran, you may qualify as an applicant for a Department of the Army nomination. (Sons and daughters of military personnel missing in action or captured may also apply for a nomination through the deceased or disabled category.) Moreover, if you are the child of a Medal of Honor recipient and meet West Point's requirements, you will be admitted to the academy.

Foreign students who wish to enroll in the academy must send their requests to the United States Defense Attaché in their country. They must also be nominated by their own government. No more than 40 foreign citizens among the four classes may be enrolled in the academy at the same time.

Taking the ACT or SAT

All applicants to the academy are required to take either the American College Testing Assessment Program exam (ACT) or the College Board Admissions Testing Program (ATP) Scholastic Aptitude Test (SAT). These tests are offered during the junior and senior years in high school and should be prepared for well in advance.

To find out when and where the next ACT exam will be held in your area, contact your high school guidance counselor or write to ACT Registration, P.O. Box 414, Iowa City, IA 52243. To ensure that the academy receives your exam results, mark the USMA's college code number on your ACT registration folder. If you wish to have a sealed copy of your scores sent to a member of Congress, also write his or her code number on your folder.

When taking the SAT, mark the academy's code number on your registration form to ensure that West Point receives your score. Again, if you want a copy of your scores sent to your congressional representatives, obtain their College Board ATP code numbers before taking the test and record them on your registration form. Direct your queries about the SAT to College Board ATP, CN 6200, Princeton, NJ 08541-6200.

Medical and Physical Exams

As stated earlier, you must meet stringent medical requirements before entering the academy. These requirements include specific height, weight, vision, and hearing standards. The qualifying medical exam, offered usually in June, is a thorough examination of your present and past state of health. Candidates do not need to travel to West Point to take the exam—it is offered at centers across the country and at some military bases overseas.

Before taking the exam, you should compile a complete medical history, noting all accidents, operations, illnesses, and injuries. Be aware that West Point will not accept an examination from your private physician. Only examinations given by authorized military personnel pass muster. The tests are scheduled and administered by the Department of Defense.

The academy's physical aptitude exam consists of four events: pull-ups for men or the flexed-arm hang for women, the standing long jump, basketball throw (for distance), and the shuttle run. West Point officials advise you to practice for the events and to build stamina through general conditioning exercises such as running.

Final Preparation before Enrollment

Your USMA file will be evaluated when you have completed the appropriate steps. Some candidates receive notice of acceptance or rejection quite early, while others may have to wait until just before July 1, the start of the academy's year.

Officials of West Point also emphasize the need to prepare yourself mentally for the strenuous programs you will face as a plebe: the transition from civilian to soldier is accomplished in an extremely short period of time. To help ease your introduction to army life, the academy urges you to stay in shape and exercise your leadership skills by participating in class and community activities.

You can get further advice from the academy's network of field representatives, who, as graduates of West Point, are willing to answer questions from interested students and help guide them through the academy's admissions process. You may contact the representative nearest you through the admissions office at West Point.

2

THE U.S. NAVAL ACADEMY AT ANNAPOLIS

Background Information

Reminders of our naval heritage surround students of the United States Naval Academy in Annapolis, Maryland. Indeed, the academy's chapel is the final resting place of John Paul Jones, Revolutionary hero and "father" of the United States Navy. The father of the naval academy itself is George Bancroft, who supervised the birth of

Located on the Severn River, the U.S. Naval Academy is a college for young men and women who want to become Navy or Marine Corps officers.
(Official U.S. Naval Academy Photograph)

The U.S. Naval Academy seal bears the motto ''Ex Scientia Tridens'' *(From knowledge, sea power)*. The seal depicts a hand grasping a trident, a shield bearing an ancient galley ready for action, and an open book. (Official U.S. Naval Academy Photograph)

the original "Naval School" built in 1845 on 10 acres surrounding Fort Severn. Today the naval academy covers 322 acres, mostly land reclaimed from the Severn River. Several acres are occupied by Bancroft Hall, a dormitory complex that houses the entire student body.

The student body is organized into the Brigade of Midshipmen, led by the commandant of midshipmen, usually a commodore or senior Navy captain. The brigade is divided into two regiments, which are further divided into three battalions, each comprised of six companies. Senior midshipmen in their third and fourth years at the academy assume most brigade leadership posts. They work closely with the brigade officers attached to the Office of the Commandant.

Naval academy officials are quick to stress the importance of a strong sense of purpose and commitment in a freshman midshipman, or plebe. Although the academy does not insist that you dedicate yourself to a lifetime of naval service when you walk through its doors, it does expect you to complete its four-year program and serve as a commissioned officer for the next five years.

From their first day at the naval academy until the end of their plebe (freshman) year, new midshipmen undergo an intensive and unabated program of military training and indoctrination. (Official U.S. Naval Academy Photograph)

Careers in the Navy

Naval officers, like their counterparts in other branches of the armed forces, can shape the course of their careers by requesting specific land and sea assignments, dependent on the current needs of the Navy. They begin that process with their initial choice of duty, made approximately three months before graduation from the naval academy.

The first-duty options open to graduating midshipmen typically include:

- conventionally powered surface-ship duty
- submarine or surface-ship nuclear-power training
- submarine strategic-weapon duty
- flight-officer and pilot training
- Marine Corps duty

Those graduates who choose surface-ship duty as their initial assignment attend the Surface Warfare Officer School for four months before reporting to their assigned ship. Midshipmen who are not physically qualified for unrestricted line-of-duty service, or who prefer to serve in a restricted field such as engineering, may opt for such diverse areas as administration, aviation maintenance, communications, cryptology, geophysics, intelligence, medicine, salvage and rescue, special warfare, and supply. Class standing and personal qualifications also help determine which routes a midshipman takes.

A naval academy graduate may eventually advance to command of an aviation squadron, surface ship, submarine, or a Marine Corps combat unit. One out of six midshipmen in each graduating class may apply for a commission as a Marine Corps second lieutenant.

Those graduates who accept Marine Corps commissions receive 21 weeks of "familiarization training" from Marine Corps officers at the basic school before moving on to formal training in their chosen specialty. These specialties include artillery, communications, data processing, engineering, infantry, intelligence, logistics, supply, and tanks. Graduates who complete the 21-week basic school program and subsequent specialty training are assigned to Fleet Marine Force operational units in the United States or abroad.

A midshipman's education does not end with graduation from the naval academy or one of the Navy's specialty schools. The need for well-rounded, educated officers continues to open new doors to education in the Marine Corps and Regular Navy. Both provide officers with opportunities for further education at the graduate level, both in military and civilian institutions.

Officers may initially receive special technical and functional training in such areas as electronics-maintenance and nuclear-power training, but after completing their first tour of duty many officers get orders for graduate-level work in economics, management, and international relations.

Life at the Academy

Once you are accepted as a midshipman you face four years of rigorous training in all areas of your life. In addition to the demands the naval academy places on your mind

After graduation and commissioning, the new Navy ensigns and Marine Corps second
lieutenants throw their midshipman hats into the air.
(Official U.S. Naval Academy Photograph)

and body, it has an honor code—*I shall not lie, cheat, or steal, nor tolerate those who
do*—that it expects all midshipmen to abide by.

During the academic year midshipmen are kept busy with scholastic and athletic activities. In the summer they undergo additional military training. Upperclassmen, for
example, spend the summer engaged in a series of sea cruises with active Navy units
or participate in various shore duties.

New midshipmen are immediately challenged by a year-long period of indoctrination designed to help them exercise self-discipline, organize their time more effectively, and think and react quickly under stress. During their plebe summer,
midshipmen are taught the basics of seamanship and signaling. They are put through
infantry drills, learn to sail a Navy yawl, and operate a minesweeping launch.

The academic year begins in late August when upperclassmen return from summer
sea duty. Midshipmen are occupied by their studies until Christmas, when they receive leave to visit their families for the holidays.

In March after mid-terms are completed, plebes begin choosing their majors. At least
80 percent of the midshipmen must major in engineering, math, or science. The remaining 20 percent may major in the humanities if they choose. All midshipmen, how-

The 49-foot Palmer Johnson sloop "Constellation," one of the academy's sailboats used for racing and training on Chesapeake Bay. (Official U.S. Naval Academy Photograph)

ever, must meet minimum course requirements in mathematics, science, social science, and the humanities.

Most midshipmen, like civilian college students, do not know when they are admitted which course of study they want to pursue. However, most do have a general idea of which field they want to enter. By the end of their plebe year they have been introduced to college-level academics and know what that experience entails. They then choose from a variety of majors including aerospace engineering, electrical engineering, marine engineering, naval architecture, ocean engineering, computer science, chemistry, oceanography, physics, English, history, economics, and political science.

After choosing a major and completing final exams, plebe midshipmen are granted a short leave. They then return for graduation and the beginning of their second year, when they become third class midshipmen. The first item on their schedule is a month of training at sea alongside first class midshipmen. This is often the first opportunity they have to work directly with enlisted men, whose respect they must earn to lead effectively. While at sea, midshipmen stand deck, engineering, gunnery, and operations watches, operate their ship's boats, and participate in shipboard drills.

In the third class year, which begins in August, midshipmen concentrate on their chosen majors. The following summer they receive more military training with the fo-

Midshipmen gathering for dress parade on historic Worden Field. The chapel is in the
background. (Official U.S. Naval Academy Photograph)

cus placed on Navy and Marine Corps operations along the East Coast, with special courses in submarine operations at the naval facilities in New London, Connecticut.

Second class midshipmen are selected to lead the brigade during the absence of first class midshipmen. They pursue more military studies and continue to progress in their majors. Second class midshipmen also play an important part in plebe indoctrination.

During their first class year, midshipmen go to sea to act as junior officers with the fleet. Those who desire a Marine Corps commission train in Hawaii and Camp Pendleton, California. At sea, first class midshipmen learn the ropes while visiting such places as Australia, Denmark, Gibraltar, Greece, Hawaii, Hong Kong, Norway, and Spain.

On their return to shore and academic life, first classmen lead the Brigade of Midshipmen in ceremonies, parades, and all daily activities. In May comes graduation and their commissions as officers in the Marine Corps or Regular Navy.

Social Life

You should not get the impression that life at Annapolis is an endless round of military training and classroom study. Midshipmen have free time and earn more of it as they progress. In fact, naval academy officials insist that all midshipmen have ample opportunity to lead a fulfilling and active social life, one that will contribute to their personal and professional growth.

Midshipmen are granted leave on a regular basis depending on their seniority, duties, and performance. They receive three weeks of leave at Christmas, mid-term leaves, and a short leave between the end of the second semester and graduation ceremonies. Members of the three upper classes get a month-long summer leave.

During the academic year midshipmen may be granted liberty in Annapolis. Plebes are granted liberty on Saturday afternoons and evenings. They may also get permission to dine off campus with family, officers, faculty, and others on weekends. However, they are permitted to date only during commissioning week and on four other weekends a year. Other class midshipmen receive liberty on Saturday afternoons, evenings, and Sunday afternoons. First classmen also have liberty on weekday afternoons and Friday evenings if it does not interfere with their academic schedule. Weekend liberty is limited to third, second, and first class midshipmen.

Much of the academy's social life is tied to sports. All members of the brigade are expected to attend Navy football games when the team plays at home. Intramural sports, the academy believes, also help reinforce bonds of friendship and build team spirit and competitiveness. The academy's several club-level teams compete against Army teams and college teams from the East Coast.

Other activities also share the limelight at Annapolis. The English department sponsors a cultural affairs program that provides midshipmen with a chance to travel to Washington, D.C. and Baltimore to attend opera, plays, concerts, and other cultural events. More than 75 extracurricular societies and clubs flourish at the academy. All activities, whether defined as professional, academic, athletic, musical, or simply recreational, are supported and run by the midshipmen.

One professional activity is the Semper Fidelis Club, which unites midshipmen interested in the Marine Corps. Those drawn to aviation may join the Flying Club, which offers training for a pilot's license. The Sportsmen's Club is cast in a more recreational mold. Its activities include club-sponsored hiking trips, hunting, fishing, camping, backpacking, and skeet shooting expeditions. Those interested in drama, music,

Midshipmen play lacrosse on both intramural and varsity levels. (Official U.S. Naval Academy Photograph)

or journalism may join the Masqueraders, a theater group that puts on two major plays a year; the contemporary ensemble Trident Brass or other bands; or they may write for the various brigade publications.

Women at the Academy

In 1975 Congress passed legislation enabling women to attend the service academies. Today women routinely compete with men for admission to the naval academy. However, the number of authorized appointments available to women is limited and fluctuates each year.

Under federal law female graduates may not be assigned to combat duty, but they do go to sea as officers on ships that do not run combat missions. Most female officers opt for on-shore careers in such fields as communications, administration, computer science, environmental science, and engineering. Some choose the Marine Corps, in which they perform all duties but infantry, artillery, tanks, and aviation.

How to Apply for Admission

Gaining admission to the naval academy is not easy. It takes years of preparation to build the academic and all-around athletic and social record of a successful applicant. Students interested in the academy should begin preparing themselves well before their senior year.

The academy recommends you pursue a college-preparatory course in high school. The curriculum urged by Navy officials includes four years of mathematics, four years of English, two years of a foreign language, one year of American, European, or world history, one year of chemistry, and one year of physics. Approximately 80 percent of the typical class of midshipmen are in the top 20 percent of their high school class.

Annapolis requires all applicants to fill out a precandidate questionnaire in the spring of their junior year. A candidate preadmission file is opened for the applicant when the questionnaire arrives at the academy. By summer, initial evaluations have been sent to all applicants. The naval academy uses information from the file to keep members of Congress informed of the status of applicants from their constituencies.

Applicants can learn more about admissions from the staff of the Candidate Guidance Office, located in Leahy Hall in Annapolis. From that office a network of Naval Reserve officers and other designated personnel branches out to serve as local counselors for the young men and women competing for admission. Those interested are encouraged to visit the guidance office in Annapolis. No appointment is necessary.

All applicants must take either the Scholastic Aptitude Test (SAT) administered by the College Board Admissions Testing Program or the American College Testing Assessment Program Exam (ACT). The academy urges students to take their chosen test in their junior year so that test data can be processed quickly and candidates evaluated more rapidly. If you plan to apply for a congressional nomination to the academy, your test results must be sent to your representative in Congress. Be sure to mark the proper code numbers for your representatives and the academy on your test folders or registration forms during the exam.

Your high school guidance counselor can tell you when and where the next test is being given in your area. You can also get information on the tests by writing directly to the Registration Department, ACT Assessment Program, or the College Board Admissions Testing Program. For both addresses, see page 13.

Applying for a Nomination

Getting a nomination is the next step toward admission to the naval academy. Nominations should be sought in the spring of your junior year so that they can be processed and returned to you as soon as possible. Nominations to the naval academy may be obtained from several sources:

- **members of Congress,** who may nominate 10 candidates for each vacancy at the naval academy; however, each member of Congress is limited to five midshipmen attending Annapolis in the four-year period;
- **the President,** who may nominate up to 100 candidates annually from among the children of career officers, enlisted personnel serving in any branch of the armed forces, and retired career personnel;

- **the Vice President,** who may nominate candidates from anywhere in the United States; however, the total number of midshipmen among the four classes nominated by the Vice President is limited to five;
- **the governor of Puerto Rico,** who may nominate 10 candidates for each vacancy at Annapolis, but no more than one midshipman nominated by the governor may attend the academy at a time; the governor may nominate only residents of Puerto Rico;
- **the resident commissioner of Puerto Rico,** who is allowed to nominate 10 candidates per vacancy and may have up to five midshipmen attending the naval academy at the same time.

In addition to those officials, the administrator of the Panama Canal Zone and delegates to Congress from Guam, the Virgin Islands, and American Samoa may each nominate 10 candidates per vacancy and have one nominee among the four classes.

Enlisted members of the Regular Navy or Marine Corps who have been on active duty for a year may apply for a nomination through their commanding officers. Members of the Naval and Marine Corps Reserves may also receive appointments. The naval academy accepts 85 midshipmen annually from the regular and reserve forces. Students enrolled in honor naval and military schools may be nominated by their headmasters; 10 of them are accepted annually.

Children of deceased or disabled veterans also receive special consideration. The sons and daughters of servicemen who were killed in action or who died during active duty are eligible for appointments, as are the children of current prisoners of war, those missing in action, and Medal of Honor recipients.

Members of Congress may follow any of three methods when nominating their 10 candidates:

1) one applicant is selected as their principal nominee and the remaining nominees designated sequentially starting with first alternate
2) a principal candidate is selected for nomination and the remaining nine candidates declared competitive alternates in no specific order
3) 10 competitors are nominated for the vacancy without a principal candidate selected

Alternates who aren't initially selected still have a chance to be appointed to Annapolis. As many as several hundred alternates who may have been passed over in the first round are accepted each year, thus ensuring that fully qualified candidates are admitted when room is available.

Naval Academy Preparatory School

Nominees who do not receive appointments may also enter the naval academy preparatory school in Newport, Rhode Island. Those nominees accepted by the preparatory school are enlisted in the Naval Reserve and attend the school with both enlisted members of the Regular Navy and Marine Corps as well as other reserve members.

The school's curriculum includes college-preparatory courses in chemistry, English, physics, and mathematics. Advanced students may take freshman-year college courses.

The U.S. Naval Academy was designated a U.S. National Historic Landmark in 1963.
(Official U.S. Naval Academy Photograph)

Medical and Physical Examinations

All candidates must meet the naval academy's physical and medical standards before being admitted. While those standards are high, academy officials note that fit applicants with normal vision rarely have trouble passing the test, which is conducted at examining centers designated by the Department of Defense Medical Examination Review Board. (Private examinations by family physicians are not acceptable.) The board schedules and evaluates the exams for Annapolis and the other service academies. The examining centers are located throughout the country and at overseas military bases. You should bring your complete medical history with information on all accidents, operations, illnesses, and injuries.

The next test each candidate must pass is the academy's physical aptitude examination. The exam consists of four separate tests measuring a candidate's agility, coordination, endurance, speed, and strength: (1) pull-ups for men or the flexed-arm hang for women; (2) a 90-inch long jump for men and 72-inch jump for women; (3) a 66-foot basketball throw for men and a 36-foot throw for women; (4) a 60.3-second shuttle run for men and a 72.6-second run for women. Points are awarded for each event, and a candidate's score must total at least 100 points.

The naval academy advises candidates to prepare for the exam well in advance through a sustained program of exercise.

Naval ROTC

There is yet another way for students to work toward a commission in the Navy or Marine Corps. The Naval Reserve Officers Training Corps (NROTC) was established in 1926 to offer students outside the academy a chance at a commission. The program burgeoned after World War II when the demand for naval officers began to grow.

The highly competitive NROTC program allows students to work toward a commission in the Regular Navy or Marine Corps while attending specified colleges across the country. Students are appointed midshipmen in the Naval Reserve and receive payment for tuition, textbooks, instructional or tutorial fees, and a monthly subsistence allowance. They arrange for their own college enrollment and room and board.

Students must also undergo military training during the summer, wear uniforms, and conduct themselves in a military manner at all times. Their commander is either a Navy captain or commander or Marine Corps colonel on the college faculty.

3

THE AIR FORCE ACADEMY

Background Information

The United States Air Force is one of the youngest branches of the armed forces. Although the United States has used pilots and planes in combat since World War I, there was no distinct air force until Congress passed a law establishing one in 1947. The leaders of the new service immediately saw a need for an academy that would train career officers and established the United States Air Force Academy, now located in Colorado Springs, Colorado.

Air Force academy graduates have a five-year service obligation. Most graduates (about 73 percent, according to recent estimates) choose flying assignments. The academy offers flight-training programs for potential pilots and navigators at air training command bases. Cadet pilot and navigator trainees may specialize in bomber, fighter, or transport planes. Graduates continue advanced training and are assigned to a combat or mission support unit.

Other Air Force career options include engineering, scientific, and technical support. The Air Force Specialty Code (AFSC) areas open to graduates of the academy include administration, audiovisual services, cartography, finance, health services, human resources, law, management, maintenance, medicine (2 percent of each graduating class may enter medical school), public affairs, special investigations, and supply.

The Cadet Wing

When entering the Air Force academy you become a member of the Cadet Wing, the military organization formed by the academy's student body. The wing is divided into 40 squadrons, each with approximately 110 cadets. The squadrons are organized into four groups, led by the commandant of cadets, an Air Force brigadier general. The general heads a military staff that provides constant leadership counseling to the senior cadets who run the wing on a daily basis.

Each new member of the wing is expected to live by the academy's honor code—*We will not lie, steal, or cheat nor tolerate among us anyone who does.* The code is meant to infuse new cadets with the courage, integrity, confidence, and responsibility the Air Force requires of professional officers.

Adherence to the code is monitored by the cadet honor committee and, most importantly, by the cadets themselves. In addition to the honor code, the academy offers several courses in ethics to develop an emotionally mature, self-reliant, and trustworthy professional officer.

Upon their arrival in Colorado Springs, new cadets are issued classroom, dress, mess

Located at the base of the Rocky Mountains, the U.S. Air Force Academy stands out in dramatic contrast to its physical environs. (Courtesy U.S. Air Force Academy)

dress, and parade dress uniforms and military fatigues, paid for with savings gleaned from their salaries. First-year, or fourth class, cadets are paid $60 a month after expenses. Second-, third-, and fourth-year cadets earn $480 a month, from which taxes, social security, and service charges are deducted. Cadets are not charged for their education, room and board, or medical care.

As a cadet you are required to complete the academy's instruction program, accept a commission as a second lieutenant in the Regular Air Force, and meet a five-year service obligation. If you are allowed to resign before the sixth anniversary of your graduation from the academy, you must serve as an Air Force Reserve officer until that time. Furthermore, if you are discharged from the academy before graduating, you may be asked to serve as an enlisted member of the Regular Air Force for up to four years.

The academy supports more than 75 cadet-managed clubs and organizations, including the Sabre Drill Team, the Science Fiction and Fantasy Club, and a Cadet Wing newspaper, yearbook, and magazine. The activities foster professional interests and provide an outlet for cadets' creative talents.

Women at the Academy

Since they first entered in 1976, women have played an increasingly important role as Air Force officers. At that time 157 women enrolled in the academy, and the first co-ed class graduated in 1980. Air Force officials stress that women perform as well as men in all areas of cadet activity. Each year a significant number of women make the dean's list and the commandant's list, which recognizes military achievement.

Military Training

The academy's fundamental mission is to train cadets to be professional military officers. Cadets enter the armed forces as soon as they arrive on the academy's campus and take the oath of allegiance. Their military life begins in their first summer term with basic military training.

Basic cadet training (BCT) that summer involves two separate stages. The first part takes place at the academy and completes the transition from civilian to military life. Senior cadets instruct new cadets in the military requirements of the academy. Testing, drilling, parades, and inspections are all part of the initial phase of BCT. The daily training regimen includes rigorous physical exercise, especially running and competitive sports.

The second part of the BCT program is held in Jack's Valley, a wilderness area on the academy's property. The training in Jack's Valley puts cadets into the field using firearms, gaining practical experience in small-unit tactics, and learning the basics of air base defense. The program ends with a field day that pits cadets against each other in such events as competitive races, a log relay, and tug of war. BCT also includes cadets' first aviation training. Cadets are introduced to airmanship through orientation flights in helicopters, Cessna T-41 planes, and a jet navigation trainer.

Cadet military training continues for four years during the summer, fall, and spring terms under the academy's professional military training (PMT) program. In the fourth class year PMT focuses on instilling professional values in each cadet. Air Force regulations and the service's heritage are the primary subjects studied.

Second-year (third class) PMT focuses on leadership training. During their third class summer cadets undergo training at the academy and in the Rocky Mountains. Participation in either of two training programs is mandatory:

- CONUS field trip: a one-week program conducted on Air Force bases that introduces cadets to operational missions
- the Soar-For-All program: instruction in dual and solo flights in Air Force academy sailplanes

The academy offers extensive training programs for potential pilots and navigators.
(Courtesy U.S. Air Force Academy)

Leadership training continues in the second class year when senior cadets are expected to help train new cadets in BCT. Second class cadets instruct newcomers in navigation, parachuting, soaring, and survival. They also take part in Operation Air Force, a three-week program held on Air Force bases worldwide.

Cadets assume top leadership positions in the Cadet Wing and BCT during their first class year. A number of optional training courses are available to them in their first class summer, including parachuting, pilot training, and navigation. During the academic year first class PMT centers on the application of leadership skills learned during the previous three years.

Military Studies

The academy also offers an academic program that concentrates on military heritage and the application of military skills. The commandant's program in professional military studies (PMS) comprises four core courses spread over four years.

The fourth class course examines the structure of the United States' military organization: the application of air power, the organization of the Air Force, its role in carrying out American military objectives, and the responsibilities of an officer. The third class course uses case studies to explore air power employment and doctrine. Second class PMS features a war-game exercise to illustrate the workings of joint staff planning and the integration of services on the modern battlefield. The final PMS course provides further instruction in military theory and looks at the military organization of foreign nations, concentrating on the Soviet Union and its allies.

Aviation Training

Providing cadets, even those who will not become pilots, with a strong background in aviation is vital to the Air Force academy's mission. Aviation training begins in BCT

Every cadet is provided with a strong background in aviation.
(Courtesy U.S. Air Force Academy)

and continues over the next four years. A course in Air Force flight activities is required of all fourth class cadets. Cadets experience simulator rides, a flight mission to an Air Force base, and classroom instruction. Advanced courses provide instruction in navigation and avionic systems. Cadets slated to fly go on to pilot training after graduating from BCT.

Academic Program

The academy's academic program is designed to provide cadets with the broad education in the arts and sciences required of an Air Force officer. First-year cadets are given a series of placement/validation tests conducted by the academy's academic departments. The test results help academy administrators place the new cadets in the appropriate first-semester courses.

During their first two years at the academy, cadets take a variety of core courses. After their third semester they are required to choose between a major and non-major track. Cadets may also choose among interdisciplinary, disciplinary, or divisional majors with different semester-hour requirements. To graduate with a disciplinary or interdisciplinary major, cadets must complete 37 core courses and nine major courses.

Academic programs at the academy are rigorous, and cadets are offered broad courses of study in the arts and sciences. (Courtesy U.S. Air Force Academy)

The academy offers four divisional majors: basic sciences, general engineering, humanities, and social sciences. Those choosing not to major in a specific field must complete the basic academic program comprising all core courses and eight electives. Faculty advisors are available to help cadets with academic decisions.

Cadets with high grades or valuable experience may enhance their collegiate education through the academy's honors and enrichment programs. The honors program is open to cadets with a minimum grade point average of 3.0, although students with lower cumulative GPAs may be admitted under special circumstances. Interdisciplinary honors seminars are also offered regularly.

The enrichment program allows cadets with previous college experience to transfer credits for equivalent courses taken at other institutions. Cadets may also use either validation exams or College Board Advanced Placement Tests to earn credit for knowledge gained in high school honors courses. Cadets who advance quickly may be enrolled in accelerated courses that fit a two-course sequence into one semester.

The academy also offers cadets opportunities to study abroad and at other United States service academies. It maintains short-term exchange programs with a number of foreign air force academies, including those of Argentina, Australia, Belgium, Brazil, Canada, Great Britain, Japan, Mexico, the Netherlands, Portugal, Saudi Arabia, Spain, and West Germany. A semester-long exchange program is offered at the École de l'Air (French air force academy). Cadets may attend another United States service academy for a semester through the interservice exchange program. Such an experience contributes to a better understanding of the entire American military establishment and promotes cooperation and uniformity among the services.

Athletics

Physical fitness is an important prerequisite for admission to the Air Force academy. Applicants must pass the candidate fitness test and will also find that the challenges posed by BCT and subsequent military training require excellent physical conditioning. Air Force academy officials view athletics as critical to the development of confidence, initiative, team spirit, self-control, and courage in each cadet, and encourage the development of those qualities through a strenuous four-year athletic program.

The academy has a number of athletic facilities. First is the cadet gymnasium, which contains three full-size gym areas; an Olympic-size pool and a 40-yard pool; basketball, handball, racquetball, tennis, and squash courts; and a rifle and pistol range. An ice rink, a basketball court ringed by 6,000 seats, and a track are located in the field house. In addition, the academy boasts 143 acres of outdoor sports fields and two entire golf courses.

The athletic program is divided among mandatory physical education, which has required courses and electives, and combative and noncombative sports; intramurals; and intercollegiate athletics. (Cadets who are not participating in intercollegiate athletics or authorized athletic clubs are required to enter the intramural program, which centers on teamwork.)

The first-year physical education program begins with BCT's steady regimen of conditioning exercises. The fall-term instruction concentrates on developing self-confidence, endurance, and upper body strength. Cadets who do not pass the academy's swimming test receive remedial instruction. Air Force officials strongly advise applicants to learn to swim before coming to the academy.

Combative courses are introduced during the second year. The second-year program also features tennis and racquet sports. A course in aerobic fitness is required for women, and wrestling for men.

Judo is one of the main courses in the third-year program. A water survival course consists of simulated disasters and emergencies that cadets may encounter as professional officers. Basic golf is another featured sport in the third-year program.

The fourth year continues with volleyball and physical conditioning. Unarmed hand-to-hand combat instruction completes the combat-oriented portion of the program.

The intramural program is administered entirely by cadets. All 40 squadrons in the Cadet Wing have an intramural team for each of the 18 intramural sports played at the academy. In the fall cadets compete in cross country, soccer, softball, tackle football, and tennis. Winter intramurals feature basketball, boxing, bowling, handball, swimming, squash, and wrestling. The spring season includes flag football, racquetball, rugby, team handball, volleyball, and water polo.

The intercollegiate program permits cadets to compete with athletes from other colleges through membership in the NCAA, Western Athletic Conference, Continental Divide Conference, and other regional leagues. Intercollegiate sports, like intramural sports, are divided among the fall, winter, and spring seasons. Fall offerings include cross country, football, soccer, tennis, volleyball, and water polo. The winter schedule features basketball, fencing, gymnastics, ice hockey, indoor track, pistol, rifle, swimming, and wrestling. Baseball, golf, lacrosse, tennis, and track are played in the spring.

Most sports are coeducational, but in the intercollegiate program volleyball is played by women only, and only men are permitted to compete in baseball, football, ice hockey, lacrosse, soccer, water polo, and wrestling.

Admissions Procedures

Air Force academy admission standards are high, and having your nomination accepted by the admissions office is a major accomplishment. Approximately ten thousand students apply to the academy each year. Of those perhaps four thousand are qualified to receive nominations, and about fifteen hundred may actually receive appointments and enter the academy. Applicants are judged on the basis of their academic, athletic, and medical records and their potential leadership abilities. The academy recommends that you begin preparing your application as early as junior high school if possible by participating in school and community activities.

An academic high school curriculum will best prepare you for the challenges you will meet at the academy. The recommended course of study includes four years of English and a concentration in algebra, functional analysis and analytical geometry, trigonometry, computer science, biology, chemistry, and physics, and two or three years of a foreign language.

Physical preparation is important, too. A personal program to increase your upper body strength, swimming ability, and endurance is recommended in addition to participation in high school sports programs. Admissions officers will evaluate your leadership qualities as demonstrated in your athletic and nonathletic high school and civic records.

Before applying to the academy, make sure you meet its eligibility requirements. You must be:

- at least 17, but not more than 21 years old

Traditional military discipline and form are espoused at the Academy.
(Courtesy U.S. Air Force Academy)

- a United States citizen
- of sound moral character
- single, without dependents

The academy also requires you to take and perform well on either the Scholastic Aptitude Test (SAT) or American College Testing Assessment Program Exam (ACT).

SAT and ACT Exams

To ensure that the Air Force academy admissions office receives your ACT scores, fill in the academy's college code number on your registration folder before taking the test. If you want sealed copies of your score sent to your representatives in Congress, add their code numbers onto your folder. For more information on ACT testing in your area, contact your high school guidance counselor or write to ACT Registration, P.O. Box 414, Iowa City, IA 52243.

Similar procedures should be followed when taking the SAT. To send a copy of your score to the academy, mark its code number on your registration form along with the code numbers of selected members of Congress if desired. SAT information is available from College Board ATP, CN 6200, Princeton, NJ 08541-6200.

Precandidate Questionnaires

Before January 31 of your high school junior year you should request a precandidate questionnaire from the academy's admissions office at HQ USAFA/RRS, United States Air Force Academy, Colorado Springs, CO 80840. The admissions office must receive the completed questionnaire before it will consider you an official candidate. The questionnaires are also used to provide members of Congress with information on applicants seeking congressional nominations.

As admissions officers evaluate your high school record, they break it down into different sections which when combined yield a "whole person" score. The academic section is based on your ACT or SAT scores and high school academic record, with special attention given to math grades and honors credits. The leadership section measures nonacademic criteria, especially athletics and civic activities.

Precandidate questionnaires should be returned to the admissions office by no later than January 31 of the year you plan to enter the academy. The academy's nationwide network of liaison officers is available to assist applicants in completing the forms. The liaison officers are in almost constant contact with the academy and can help candidates with any problems they might encounter during the admissions process.

Once the questionnaires have been thoroughly evaluated, the admissions office will let you know whether you meet the Air Force academy's criteria. If you don't, you may reapply at a later time. If you do qualify, officials urge you to concentrate on obtaining a nomination to the academy.

Getting a Nomination

Obtaining a nomination is usually time consuming, and the academy recommends you begin the process early in your junior year when sending for your precandidate questionnaire. Make sure you apply in every category for which you are eligible.

The first category includes nominations from members of Congress. Senators and representatives may have no more than five of their nominees among the four cadet classes. When one of those cadets graduates, creating a vacancy, a member may nominate up to 10 candidates to fill the spot. You must seek a nomination from the senators from your state and the representative from your congressional district.

Members of Congress may nominate candidates through three different methods:

1. the principal/alternate method, in which one candidate is designated the principal nominee and is accepted if he or she meets the academy's standards; the other candidates are ranked as alternates in a predetermined order of preference;
2. the principal/competitive method, which is identical to the previous method except that alternates are judged on a competitive rather than a preferential basis;
3. the fully competitive method, in which all candidates compete openly for the nomination and no candidate is designated as principal.

Congressional delegates from the District of Columbia, the island of Guam, the U.S. Virgin Islands, and American Samoa, along with the Panama Canal commission administrator and the resident commissioner and governor of Puerto Rico, may also use these methods to nominate candidates.

Nominations are also made by the Vice President, whose applicants may come from anywhere in the United States. The President may nominate children of career military personnel. In order for you to qualify for a presidential nomination a parent must be on active duty for at least eight years or be retired with pay or be granted such pay. You are also eligible if you are the son or daughter of deceased career personnel.

The children of parents who are missing or were killed in action may apply for nominations as the children of either missing military or civilian personnel or of deceased or disabled veterans. In addition, the children of Medal of Honor recipients may receive appointments if they meet the academy's eligibility requirements.

Airmen in the Regular Air Force, Air Force Reserve, and Air Force National Guard may apply for nominations through official channels. Also, five students from each college and university Air Force Reserve Training Officer Corps unit may be nominated per year. Students in honor military and naval schools approved by the academy may also apply.

Standards for foreign students applying to the academy are high: they must speak, read, and write English; complete either the SAT or ACT exam; and must be nominated by an official of their government. Foreign students may not receive Air Force commissions. The academy permits up to 40 foreign students to attend at one time, and no country may have more than three cadets at the academy simultaneously.

Medical and Physical Exams

The Air Force academy uses the standardized medical examination accepted by all United States service academies. The academy does not administer the exam directly, but accepts the results from designated military examining centers located throughout the country and on some military bases overseas. Before they are sent to the academy, those test results are forwarded to the Department of Defense Medical Examination Review Board, which evaluates them and makes final recommendations to the Air Force.

Examinations performed by family doctors are not accepted, but private dental examinations are encouraged, and women may have private physicians perform the pelvic examination and Pap test required by the admissions office.

The Air Force has some specific medical requirements: All candidates must take a cycloplegic (visual) test to determine their flying status. Candidates with hard contact lenses must take them out at least 21 days before the visual tests; soft lens users must remove theirs at least three days before the tests. (Air Force personnel are forbidden to wear contact lenses while flying.) Nearsightedness is a common visual problem that prevents candidates from qualifying for pilot training.

You must take the examinations on or after June 1 of the year prior to admission. The examiners will also require a full medical history, which can be provided by your family physician. All illnesses, operations, injuries, and accidents should be included.

The candidate fitness test (CFT) is the next hurdle you must overcome on the road to an appointment. The test measures agility, coordination, endurance, speed, and strength and is given only to those candidates who have received a nomination and who meet the minimum admissions criteria.

The CFT is given at examining centers across the nation. The academy makes an effort to schedule the test at centers close to candidates' homes. The CFT has four elements: pushups, situps, pullups, and the 300-yard shuttle run. Candidates are graded on their performance in each category.

Selection Procedures

The academy's candidate selection panel meets weekly beginning in November to decide which candidates will receive appointments. Candidates are appointed by the academy board, which is formed by the superintendent and his staff officers. All appointments are made at the discretion of the Secretary of the Air Force.

By mid-May all candidates have been told whether they will receive an appointment. Those who are not initially granted an appointment are placed on the qualified alternate list. They then compete for any subsequent vacancies.

Candidates who are especially qualified for appointment or who hold principal nominations may be informed of their appointment as soon as their records have been reviewed. Those candidates who do not receive early appointments are usually notified of their status in April if their records are complete. Those whose records are not completed by April 1 will be considered only for late appointments, dependent upon whether any vacancies exist.

4

THE U.S. COAST GUARD ACADEMY

Background Information

The Coast Guard grew out of the merger of the old Revenue Cutter Service, established in 1790 to keep smugglers from U.S. shores, and the Life Saving Service in 1915. Today the Coast Guard is a peacetime arm of the federal Department of Transportation. One of its greatest responsibilities is the enforcement of maritime law. Coast Guard ships are also used to enforce customs and immigration laws, combat narcotics smuggling, investigate and help prevent acts of piracy, and protect endangered species. The Coast Guard functions as an arm of the Navy during war, guarding convoys and performing dangerous rescue missions.

Before the Revenue Cutter Service merged into the Coast Guard, it operated a training program aboard revenue ships and in facilities located in New Bedford, Massachusetts, and Arundel Cove, Maryland. Since 1910, the United States Coast Guard Academy has been based in Fort Trumbull near New London, Connecticut.

Academy graduates must serve as Coast Guard officers for five years. A graduate's first assignment is at sea or on the Great Lakes. Newly commissioned officers are often assigned to icebreakers conducting scientific and logistical missions while patrolling the Arctic and Antarctic.

Both men and women have important roles to play in the maritime service. Coast Guard officials stress that women "serve aboard and command Coast Guard ships and planes."

Many graduates return to shore for postgraduate study once their first tour of sea duty is completed. According to the academy, approximately 60 percent of its graduates are selected for advanced study during their first five years of duty. Academy records also indicate that 88 percent of its graduates decide to stay with the Coast Guard after their five-year minimum service obligation is completed.

The areas of advanced study open to Coast Guard academy graduates include administrative science, both management and personnel; aeronautical engineering; computer systems management; electronics; environmental management; industrial management; law; marine engineering and naval architecture; oceanography; port safety; and transportation management, among many others.

New students automatically join the Coast Guard Corps of Cadets. The cadets are governed by the regimental commander and his staff and the commandant of cadets. Cadet life is an introduction to the military world. The skills, knowledge, and spirit needed to be a Coast Guard officer are instilled in each cadet.

Like the other service academies, the Coast Guard academy bases its instruction on a progressive four-year program that includes academics as well as military, nautical, and physical training.

The first, or fourth class, year is the hardest. Fourth class cadets must develop self-

The U.S. Coast Guard Academy, in New London, Connecticut, upholds time-honored maritime traditions. (Courtesy U.S. Coast Guard Academy)

control, discipline, and respect for authority to meet the rigorous academic and physical demands found in the transition from civilian to military life.

In the ensuing years cadets are given increased responsibility and authority until in their first class year they earn command of the Corps of Cadets. Cadets gain further experience during summers, when they participate in cruises aboard training vessels. Upperclassmen serve as officers during the cruises.

Academics

The Coast Guard academy has eight academic departments: computer science, economics and management, engineering, humanities, mathematics, nautical science, law, and physical education. Approximately 80 percent of the cadets currently graduate with degrees in technical areas.

The majors available to cadets are applied science, civil engineering, government, marine engineering, management, and mathematical sciences. Cadets are usually required to complete a core program of 26 courses, in addition to the courses included in their major, to receive the Bachelor of Science degree.

Cadets must also fulfill the requirements of the academy's physical education program, which begins with an entrance test and continues with semiannual exams. Ca-

Both men and women have important roles in maritime service.
(Courtesy U.S. Coast Guard Academy)

dets enroll in physical education courses each semester and may choose among such
subjects as survival swimming, advanced swimming, lifesaving, gymnastics, personal
defense, and first aid. Intramural or intercollegiate sports are also mandatory.

Admissions

The Coast Guard academy's admissions procedures are unique among the service
academies. Instead of requiring applicants to obtain nominations from members of

Nautical study is integral to Coast Guard training. (Courtesy U.S. Coast Guard Academy)

Congress or other officials, the academy selects its students in a nationwide competition after examining their SAT or ACT exam scores, high school transcripts, and extracurricular records.

All applicants must meet the following requirements:

- they must be at least 17 years old but no older than 22 on July 1 of the year they plan to enter the academy;
- except for foreign students nominated by their government and accepted by the coast guard academy, they must be United States citizens;
- they must be single; cadets who marry before their graduation are asked to resign and are dismissed if they refuse;
- they must prove that their moral character is sound and demonstrate that they are trustworthy, responsible citizens who will live by the academy's honor concept and *neither lie, cheat, nor attempt to deceive;*
- they must be between 5 feet and 6 feet 6 inches tall;
- they must complete a four-year high school or preparatory school program before entering the academy.

Scholastic accomplishments are measured in units that represent a year's work in any subject. Accordingly, applicants should have completed 16 units of study by the time they graduate from high school. Students must submit a transcript covering 15 units of work to be accepted as applicants.

Military, academic, and physical training is intensive. (Courtesy U.S. Coast Guard Academy)

Six units are mandatory for applicants—three of mathematics and three of English. The remaining nine may be completed in mathematics, social studies, English, biology and physics, foreign language, and other elective subjects.

Applying to the Academy

You must submit to the academy an application form available from the Coast Guard requesting permission to participate in its annual entrance competition. That nation-wide competition does not include state quotas or special categories and is open to all qualifying civilians and members of the armed forces.

Applications for the following June must be received before December 15. Once the application has been processed, the Coast Guard will send you a cadet candidate questionnaire, request for secondary school information, "school official's evaluation of candidate" forms, and the evaluation questionnaire for military personnel. These forms must be completed and returned to the academy by January 15.

Applicants must take the ACT or SAT test. Since the exam scores are an important part of the evaluation process, you should prepare carefully for the tests. You must score at least 950 on the SAT with a math score of 500 and a verbal score of 450, or a 40 on the ACT with a math score of 21, to be accepted for evaluation.

The academy's training vessels play an important part in cadets' nautical training.
(Courtesy U.S. Coast Guard Academy)

You may take either test during your junior high school year and during the fall of your senior year, but the scores of tests taken after the senior year December exams will not be considered. Make sure that your test registration forms are filled out so that copies of your test scores are sent to the academy. For more information on SAT and ACT testing in your area, contact your guidance counselor.

When selecting applicants for appointment, the cadet candidate evaluation board considers SAT and ACT scores, high school transcripts, and responses to the academy's questionnaires. The final marks of each candidate are figured by averaging test scores, academic records, and the board's own rating. Notices of appointment are usually mailed to successful applicants in April.

The last hurdles applicants must clear before being accepted to the academy are its medical examinations. First, all applicants are required to take the standard service academy medical examinations administered and analyzed by the Department of Defense Medical Examination Review Board.

The exams are conducted at armed forces medical facilities across the country and on a few military bases overseas. Medical exams conducted by private physicians or family doctors are not acceptable; only those given by authorized military medical officers are valid. Be sure to supply the military doctors with a complete medical history listing all accidents and illnesses.

5

THE U.S. MERCHANT MARINE ACADEMY

Background Information

The United States Merchant Marine Academy was established in 1938 to help provide the nation's maritime industry with high quality licensed officers to direct and command the country's private merchant fleet.

The need for such men and women is more critical today than ever before. According to the academy, more than one-third of the world's raw material output is consumed by the United States, which has 6 percent of the world's population. Most of those raw materials are brought to American ports by ship, and many of those ships are commanded by graduates of the Merchant Marine academy.

The academy is located on 80 acres of land at Kings Point, New York, on the northern shore of Long Island overlooking Long Island Sound. It is operated by the Department of Transportation but is also linked to the Navy, which may mobilize merchant officers in an emergency if necessary.

Graduating students of the merchant marine academy must choose to serve as Merchant Marine officers, employees in a maritime-related industry, or as commissioned officers in the United States armed forces or the National Oceanic and Atmospheric Administration.

Each graduate must maintain his or her license as a Merchant Marine officer for at least six years after graduating and must also serve as a commissioned officer in a reserve unit of the armed forces. Graduates are commissioned into the Merchant Marine Reserve or United States Naval Reserve as ensigns and are licensed as third mates or third assistant engineers.

The academy's students belong to the Regiment of Midshipmen, which trains men and women for their commissions as maritime officers. The regiment is divided into three battalions, each governed by a midshipman battalion commander.

The basis of regimental life is the academy's class system. Through the class system, freshmen, or plebes, are trained by sophomores, juniors, and seniors—known at Kings Point as third, second, and first classmen. First classmen, and some second classmen, are billeted as officers in the Regiment of Midshipmen and lead the plebes through their period of indoctrination.

The plebe year is the hardest year for most midshipmen. Freshmen are granted few freedoms and face many restrictions. Plebes are rarely granted overnight liberty, and their daily schedule is particularly rigorous. Academy officials, however, note that fourth classmen soon accept the duties imposed on them at Kings Point and join fully in regimental life.

Another important plank in the structure of regimental life is the Merchant Marine honor concept: *A midshipman will not lie, cheat, or steal.* The honor concept is designed to develop and strengthen a sense of integrity in each midshipman and a sense of trust and fellowship among all members of the regiment.

The U.S. Merchant Marine Academy at Kings Point, New York, overlooks Long Island Sound. (Courtesy U.S. Merchant Marine Academy)

Life at Kings Point

Midshipmen are housed in the six on-campus dormitory buildings. The Kings Point campus is designed to accommodate over 1,000 midshipmen. Most buildings at Kings Point are similar to those found on any typical college campus; there are academic and administrative buildings, a dining hall, and several athletic fields. However, the campus also has buildings with classrooms and laboratories designed for instruction in nautical science and nuclear engineering.

The National Maritime Research Center is located in Furuseth Hall. The center's mission is to coordinate and disseminate information on new maritime technologies and to test and evaluate products developed for maritime applications. Some first classmen participate in special self-directed research projects run with the aid of the center through the Kings Point scholar program. Those projects typically take the place of electives during the first class year.

The academy also houses the Computer-Aided Operations Research Facility (CAORF). Located in Samuels Hall, the CAORF features a ship-handling simulator with a full-scale bridge and a 240-degree field-of-vision screen. Research performed at

The academy offers a four-year accredited college curriculum. Midshipmen may study
nautical science, marine engineering, or a unique program that combines both areas.
(Courtesy U.S. Merchant Marine Academy)

the CAORF is also geared to improve ship performance, reduce the chance of colli-
sions and groundings, improve officer training procedures, and develop ports and improve their productivity.

The Academic Program

Midshipmen at the Merchant Marine academy are offered four academic tracks:
marine transportation, marine engineering, a dual license combination of the two tracks,
and marine engineering systems, which is a more difficult and comprehensive track than
marine engineering and is accredited by the Accrediting Board for Engineering and
Technology. Various elective courses and mandatory naval science courses are also
offered at the academy.

The academy's academic year has four quarters which together total nearly 11
months. During portions of their third and second class years, midshipmen participate

in the shipboard training program, which lasts for about five months each year. Through it, midshipmen board commercial vessels to become familiar with merchant operations at sea.

Besides performing any required shipboard duties midshipmen must complete a written project during their time at sea. The projects allow the students to apply the knowledge they have gained at the academy.

The sea project assignments are divided between nautical science and marine engineering subjects. The nautical science projects include cargo, internship, marine engineering for deck, navigation, rules of the road, seamanship, ship construction, and weather for mariners. The marine engineering projects may be deck operations for engineers, diesel engineering, electrical engineering, internship, labor relations, machine shop, marine engineering systems, marine engineering operations, naval architecture, and refrigeration and air conditioning.

A two-week shore program that provides training in shipyards, steamship companies, ship repair facilities, ship brokerage/chartering firms, port and terminal facilities, and other maritime-related areas rounds out midshipmen's practical training.

Midshipman takes an azimuth sighting during a training cruise. Midshipmen also spend one full year training at sea upon U.S.-flag merchant ships.
(Courtesy U.S. Merchant Marine Academy)

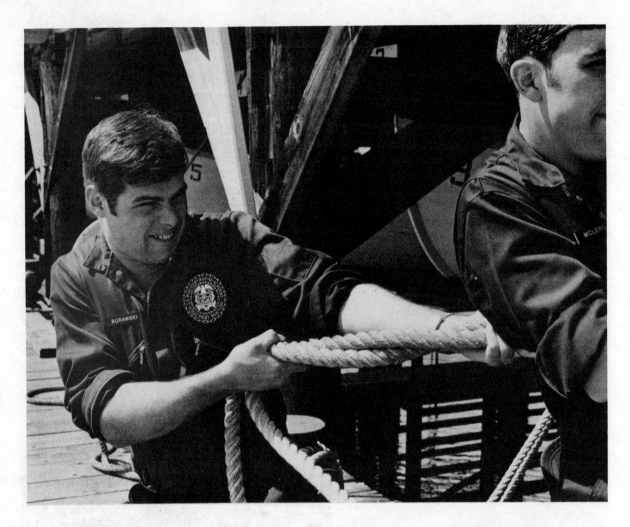

"Hands-on" training is emphasized at the academy as much as classroom theory. Here, a midshipman helps lower a lifeboat into the water. (Courtesy U.S. Merchant Marine Academy)

Merchant Marine Careers

While most of the young officers who graduate from the Merchant Marine academy will naturally seek employment aboard a commercial ship, there are other career avenues open to them.

Many find jobs onshore in port and terminal facilities practicing admiralty law or working as canal and harbor pilots or maritime surveyors. Others might find work as cargo brokers or be employed by companies engaged in offshore drilling, salvage operations, and intermodal transportation. These are only a sample of the opportunities available in the marine transportation industry.

Those who do find jobs aboard ships are placed in charge of a watch on the bridge or in the engineering room and are responsible for the ship's performance and safety during that period. After a year of service, they may take the exam for a second mate's or second assistant engineer's license. After a year as second mate or assistant engineer, they may take the exam for the chief mate's or first assistant engineer's license. Graduates may eventually become a ship's master or chief engineer. All licensing is done by the Coast Guard.

The academy sailing team, which has ranked first nationally in collegiate sailing in recent years, is one of 18 varsity sports available to midshipmen.
(Courtesy U.S. Merchant Marine Academy)

Admissions

The Merchant Marine academy grants appointments through a nomination system similar to those of most service academies. To gain admission each applicant must be nominated by a member of Congress from his or her state. The President and Vice President do not nominate applicants to Kings Point.

Applicants from American Samoa and the Northern Mariana Islands may be nominated by their governor or representatives in Congress. Applicants from the Commonwealth of Puerto Rico, the District of Columbia, Guam, and the Virgin Islands may be nominated by their delegates to the House of Representatives.

High school students should request a nomination from their congressional representative in the spring of their junior year. (A form letter example of a nomination request is featured on p. 12.) At the same time or soon after, students should request an application form from the academy. Once this request is received, the academy sends applicants precandidate questionnaires that should be completed and returned as soon as possible.

All applicants must complete either the College Board's Scholastic Aptitude Test (SAT) or the American College Testing Program's ACT exam. The exams, which are offered during a student's junior and senior years, should be prepared for well in advance. Results should be sent to nominating members of Congress and the academy.

To ensure that the exam results reach Kings Point and the nominating member of Congress, students must fill in the appropriate codes for the academy and their representative on the ACT registration folder or SAT form.

The medical exams applicants must pass to gain admission to the academy are scheduled and administered by the Department of Defense Medical Examination Review Board. The exams are held at facilities throughout the country and at some overseas bases. The medical review board, not the academy, decides whether an applicant is physically fit to enter the Merchant Marine.

The medical examination is thorough, covering such areas as vision, hearing, dental condition, and the heart and vascular system. It is not daunting, however, to applicants in good physical condition.

Some medical conditions will disqualify an applicant, among them anemia, abnormal bleeding, arthritis, acute communicable diseases, diabetes or a history of diabetes in both parents, severe hay fever, major joint surgery during the year before the exam or uncorrected derangement of a knee joint, ununited fractures, and personality disorders. Applicants should have a complete medical history listing all illnesses, accidents, and operations prepared for the doctors giving the exam. No waivers for any of the medical or scholastic tests required by the academy are granted.

Most applicants are notified of their appointments on or about May 1 of the year they plan to enter the academy. Outstanding candidates, however, may be notified of their appointments earlier. The sooner an outstanding candidate's application is processed, the earlier he or she will be notified of acceptance.

Candidate briefing programs that introduce students to midshipmen, faculty members, and members of the academy's administration are held each year, usually in May. All candidates are invited to attend the programs, which are voluntary.

Academy graduates receive licenses as Merchant Marine officers, Bachelor of Science
degrees, and commissions as ensigns in the U.S. Naval Reserve.
(Courtesy U.S. Merchant Marine Academy)

Part Two

Sample Entrance
Examinations

ANSWER SHEET: MODEL ACT EXAM

English Usage

1 Ⓐ Ⓑ Ⓒ Ⓓ   12 Ⓕ Ⓖ Ⓗ Ⓙ   23 Ⓐ Ⓑ Ⓒ Ⓓ   34 Ⓕ Ⓖ Ⓗ Ⓙ   45 Ⓐ Ⓑ Ⓒ Ⓓ   56 Ⓕ Ⓖ Ⓗ Ⓙ   67 Ⓐ Ⓑ Ⓒ Ⓓ
2 Ⓕ Ⓖ Ⓗ Ⓙ   13 Ⓐ Ⓑ Ⓒ Ⓓ   24 Ⓕ Ⓖ Ⓗ Ⓙ   35 Ⓐ Ⓑ Ⓒ Ⓓ   46 Ⓕ Ⓖ Ⓗ Ⓙ   57 Ⓐ Ⓑ Ⓒ Ⓓ   68 Ⓕ Ⓖ Ⓗ Ⓙ
3 Ⓐ Ⓑ Ⓒ Ⓓ   14 Ⓕ Ⓖ Ⓗ Ⓙ   25 Ⓐ Ⓑ Ⓒ Ⓓ   36 Ⓕ Ⓖ Ⓗ Ⓙ   47 Ⓐ Ⓑ Ⓒ Ⓓ   58 Ⓕ Ⓖ Ⓗ Ⓙ   69 Ⓐ Ⓑ Ⓒ Ⓓ
4 Ⓕ Ⓖ Ⓗ Ⓙ   15 Ⓐ Ⓑ Ⓒ Ⓓ   26 Ⓕ Ⓖ Ⓗ Ⓙ   37 Ⓐ Ⓑ Ⓒ Ⓓ   48 Ⓕ Ⓖ Ⓗ Ⓙ   59 Ⓐ Ⓑ Ⓒ Ⓓ   70 Ⓕ Ⓖ Ⓗ Ⓙ
5 Ⓐ Ⓑ Ⓒ Ⓓ   16 Ⓕ Ⓖ Ⓗ Ⓙ   27 Ⓐ Ⓑ Ⓒ Ⓓ   38 Ⓕ Ⓖ Ⓗ Ⓙ   49 Ⓐ Ⓑ Ⓒ Ⓓ   60 Ⓕ Ⓖ Ⓗ Ⓙ   71 Ⓐ Ⓑ Ⓒ Ⓓ
6 Ⓕ Ⓖ Ⓗ Ⓙ   17 Ⓐ Ⓑ Ⓒ Ⓓ   28 Ⓕ Ⓖ Ⓗ Ⓙ   39 Ⓐ Ⓑ Ⓒ Ⓓ   50 Ⓕ Ⓖ Ⓗ Ⓙ   61 Ⓐ Ⓑ Ⓒ Ⓓ   72 Ⓕ Ⓖ Ⓗ Ⓙ
7 Ⓐ Ⓑ Ⓒ Ⓓ   18 Ⓕ Ⓖ Ⓗ Ⓙ   29 Ⓐ Ⓑ Ⓒ Ⓓ   40 Ⓕ Ⓖ Ⓗ Ⓙ   51 Ⓐ Ⓑ Ⓒ Ⓓ   62 Ⓕ Ⓖ Ⓗ Ⓙ   73 Ⓐ Ⓑ Ⓒ Ⓓ
8 Ⓕ Ⓖ Ⓗ Ⓙ   19 Ⓐ Ⓑ Ⓒ Ⓓ   30 Ⓕ Ⓖ Ⓗ Ⓙ   41 Ⓐ Ⓑ Ⓒ Ⓓ   52 Ⓕ Ⓖ Ⓗ Ⓙ   63 Ⓐ Ⓑ Ⓒ Ⓓ   74 Ⓕ Ⓖ Ⓗ Ⓙ
9 Ⓐ Ⓑ Ⓒ Ⓓ   20 Ⓕ Ⓖ Ⓗ Ⓙ   31 Ⓐ Ⓑ Ⓒ Ⓓ   42 Ⓕ Ⓖ Ⓗ Ⓙ   53 Ⓐ Ⓑ Ⓒ Ⓓ   64 Ⓕ Ⓖ Ⓗ Ⓙ   75 Ⓐ Ⓑ Ⓒ Ⓓ
10 Ⓕ Ⓖ Ⓗ Ⓙ   21 Ⓐ Ⓑ Ⓒ Ⓓ   32 Ⓕ Ⓖ Ⓗ Ⓙ   43 Ⓐ Ⓑ Ⓒ Ⓓ   54 Ⓕ Ⓖ Ⓗ Ⓙ   65 Ⓐ Ⓑ Ⓒ Ⓓ
11 Ⓐ Ⓑ Ⓒ Ⓓ   22 Ⓕ Ⓖ Ⓗ Ⓙ   33 Ⓐ Ⓑ Ⓒ Ⓓ   44 Ⓕ Ⓖ Ⓗ Ⓙ   55 Ⓐ Ⓑ Ⓒ Ⓓ   66 Ⓕ Ⓖ Ⓗ Ⓙ

Mathematics Usage

1 Ⓐ Ⓑ Ⓒ Ⓓ Ⓔ   7 Ⓐ Ⓑ Ⓒ Ⓓ Ⓔ   13 Ⓐ Ⓑ Ⓒ Ⓓ Ⓔ   19 Ⓐ Ⓑ Ⓒ Ⓓ Ⓔ   25 Ⓐ Ⓑ Ⓒ Ⓓ Ⓔ   31 Ⓐ Ⓑ Ⓒ Ⓓ Ⓔ   37 Ⓐ Ⓑ Ⓒ Ⓓ Ⓔ
2 Ⓕ Ⓖ Ⓗ Ⓙ Ⓚ   8 Ⓕ Ⓖ Ⓗ Ⓙ Ⓚ   14 Ⓕ Ⓖ Ⓗ Ⓙ Ⓚ   20 Ⓕ Ⓖ Ⓗ Ⓙ Ⓚ   26 Ⓕ Ⓖ Ⓗ Ⓙ Ⓚ   32 Ⓕ Ⓖ Ⓗ Ⓙ Ⓚ   38 Ⓕ Ⓖ Ⓗ Ⓙ Ⓚ
3 Ⓐ Ⓑ Ⓒ Ⓓ Ⓔ   9 Ⓐ Ⓑ Ⓒ Ⓓ Ⓔ   15 Ⓐ Ⓑ Ⓒ Ⓓ Ⓔ   21 Ⓐ Ⓑ Ⓒ Ⓓ Ⓔ   27 Ⓐ Ⓑ Ⓒ Ⓓ Ⓔ   33 Ⓐ Ⓑ Ⓒ Ⓓ Ⓔ   39 Ⓐ Ⓑ Ⓒ Ⓓ Ⓔ
4 Ⓕ Ⓖ Ⓗ Ⓙ Ⓚ   10 Ⓕ Ⓖ Ⓗ Ⓙ Ⓚ   16 Ⓕ Ⓖ Ⓗ Ⓙ Ⓚ   22 Ⓕ Ⓖ Ⓗ Ⓙ Ⓚ   28 Ⓕ Ⓖ Ⓗ Ⓙ Ⓚ   34 Ⓕ Ⓖ Ⓗ Ⓙ Ⓚ   40 Ⓕ Ⓖ Ⓗ Ⓙ Ⓚ
5 Ⓐ Ⓑ Ⓒ Ⓓ Ⓔ   11 Ⓐ Ⓑ Ⓒ Ⓓ Ⓔ   17 Ⓐ Ⓑ Ⓒ Ⓓ Ⓔ   23 Ⓐ Ⓑ Ⓒ Ⓓ Ⓔ   29 Ⓐ Ⓑ Ⓒ Ⓓ Ⓔ   35 Ⓐ Ⓑ Ⓒ Ⓓ Ⓔ
6 Ⓕ Ⓖ Ⓗ Ⓙ Ⓚ   12 Ⓕ Ⓖ Ⓗ Ⓙ Ⓚ   18 Ⓕ Ⓖ Ⓗ Ⓙ Ⓚ   24 Ⓕ Ⓖ Ⓗ Ⓙ Ⓚ   30 Ⓕ Ⓖ Ⓗ Ⓙ Ⓚ   36 Ⓕ Ⓖ Ⓗ Ⓙ Ⓚ

Social Studies Reading

1 Ⓐ Ⓑ Ⓒ Ⓓ   8 Ⓕ Ⓖ Ⓗ Ⓙ   15 Ⓐ Ⓑ Ⓒ Ⓓ   22 Ⓕ Ⓖ Ⓗ Ⓙ   29 Ⓐ Ⓑ Ⓒ Ⓓ   36 Ⓕ Ⓖ Ⓗ Ⓙ   43 Ⓐ Ⓑ Ⓒ Ⓓ Ⓔ   50 Ⓕ Ⓖ Ⓗ Ⓙ Ⓚ
2 Ⓕ Ⓖ Ⓗ Ⓙ   9 Ⓐ Ⓑ Ⓒ Ⓓ   16 Ⓕ Ⓖ Ⓗ Ⓙ   23 Ⓐ Ⓑ Ⓒ Ⓓ   30 Ⓕ Ⓖ Ⓗ Ⓙ   37 Ⓐ Ⓑ Ⓒ Ⓓ   44 Ⓕ Ⓖ Ⓗ Ⓙ Ⓚ   51 Ⓐ Ⓑ Ⓒ Ⓓ Ⓔ
3 Ⓐ Ⓑ Ⓒ Ⓓ   10 Ⓕ Ⓖ Ⓗ Ⓙ   17 Ⓐ Ⓑ Ⓒ Ⓓ   24 Ⓕ Ⓖ Ⓗ Ⓙ   31 Ⓐ Ⓑ Ⓒ Ⓓ   38 Ⓕ Ⓖ Ⓗ Ⓙ   45 Ⓐ Ⓑ Ⓒ Ⓓ Ⓔ   52 Ⓕ Ⓖ Ⓗ Ⓙ Ⓚ
4 Ⓕ Ⓖ Ⓗ Ⓙ   11 Ⓐ Ⓑ Ⓒ Ⓓ   18 Ⓕ Ⓖ Ⓗ Ⓙ   25 Ⓐ Ⓑ Ⓒ Ⓓ   32 Ⓕ Ⓖ Ⓗ Ⓙ   39 Ⓐ Ⓑ Ⓒ Ⓓ   46 Ⓕ Ⓖ Ⓗ Ⓙ Ⓚ
5 Ⓐ Ⓑ Ⓒ Ⓓ   12 Ⓕ Ⓖ Ⓗ Ⓙ   19 Ⓐ Ⓑ Ⓒ Ⓓ   26 Ⓕ Ⓖ Ⓗ Ⓙ   33 Ⓐ Ⓑ Ⓒ Ⓓ   40 Ⓕ Ⓖ Ⓗ Ⓙ   47 Ⓐ Ⓑ Ⓒ Ⓓ
6 Ⓕ Ⓖ Ⓗ Ⓙ   13 Ⓐ Ⓑ Ⓒ Ⓓ   20 Ⓕ Ⓖ Ⓗ Ⓙ   27 Ⓐ Ⓑ Ⓒ Ⓓ   34 Ⓕ Ⓖ Ⓗ Ⓙ   41 Ⓐ Ⓑ Ⓒ Ⓓ   48 Ⓕ Ⓖ Ⓗ Ⓙ
7 Ⓐ Ⓑ Ⓒ Ⓓ   14 Ⓕ Ⓖ Ⓗ Ⓙ   21 Ⓐ Ⓑ Ⓒ Ⓓ   28 Ⓕ Ⓖ Ⓗ Ⓙ   35 Ⓐ Ⓑ Ⓒ Ⓓ   42 Ⓕ Ⓖ Ⓗ Ⓙ   49 Ⓐ Ⓑ Ⓒ Ⓓ Ⓔ

Natural Science Reading

1 Ⓐ Ⓑ Ⓒ Ⓓ   8 Ⓕ Ⓖ Ⓗ Ⓙ   15 Ⓐ Ⓑ Ⓒ Ⓓ   22 Ⓕ Ⓖ Ⓗ Ⓙ   29 Ⓐ Ⓑ Ⓒ Ⓓ   36 Ⓕ Ⓖ Ⓗ Ⓙ   43 Ⓐ Ⓑ Ⓒ Ⓓ Ⓔ   50 Ⓕ Ⓖ Ⓗ Ⓙ Ⓚ
2 Ⓕ Ⓖ Ⓗ Ⓙ   9 Ⓐ Ⓑ Ⓒ Ⓓ   16 Ⓕ Ⓖ Ⓗ Ⓙ   23 Ⓐ Ⓑ Ⓒ Ⓓ   30 Ⓕ Ⓖ Ⓗ Ⓙ   37 Ⓐ Ⓑ Ⓒ Ⓓ   44 Ⓕ Ⓖ Ⓗ Ⓙ Ⓚ   51 Ⓐ Ⓑ Ⓒ Ⓓ Ⓔ
3 Ⓐ Ⓑ Ⓒ Ⓓ   10 Ⓕ Ⓖ Ⓗ Ⓙ   17 Ⓐ Ⓑ Ⓒ Ⓓ   24 Ⓕ Ⓖ Ⓗ Ⓙ   31 Ⓐ Ⓑ Ⓒ Ⓓ   38 Ⓕ Ⓖ Ⓗ Ⓙ   45 Ⓐ Ⓑ Ⓒ Ⓓ Ⓔ   52 Ⓕ Ⓖ Ⓗ Ⓙ Ⓚ
4 Ⓕ Ⓖ Ⓗ Ⓙ   11 Ⓐ Ⓑ Ⓒ Ⓓ   18 Ⓕ Ⓖ Ⓗ Ⓙ   25 Ⓐ Ⓑ Ⓒ Ⓓ   32 Ⓕ Ⓖ Ⓗ Ⓙ   39 Ⓐ Ⓑ Ⓒ Ⓓ   46 Ⓕ Ⓖ Ⓗ Ⓙ Ⓚ
5 Ⓐ Ⓑ Ⓒ Ⓓ   12 Ⓕ Ⓖ Ⓗ Ⓙ   19 Ⓐ Ⓑ Ⓒ Ⓓ   26 Ⓕ Ⓖ Ⓗ Ⓙ   33 Ⓐ Ⓑ Ⓒ Ⓓ   40 Ⓕ Ⓖ Ⓗ Ⓙ   47 Ⓐ Ⓑ Ⓒ Ⓓ
6 Ⓕ Ⓖ Ⓗ Ⓙ   13 Ⓐ Ⓑ Ⓒ Ⓓ   20 Ⓕ Ⓖ Ⓗ Ⓙ   27 Ⓐ Ⓑ Ⓒ Ⓓ   34 Ⓕ Ⓖ Ⓗ Ⓙ   41 Ⓐ Ⓑ Ⓒ Ⓓ   48 Ⓕ Ⓖ Ⓗ Ⓙ Ⓚ
7 Ⓐ Ⓑ Ⓒ Ⓓ   14 Ⓕ Ⓖ Ⓗ Ⓙ   21 Ⓐ Ⓑ Ⓒ Ⓓ   28 Ⓕ Ⓖ Ⓗ Ⓙ   35 Ⓐ Ⓑ Ⓒ Ⓓ   42 Ⓕ Ⓖ Ⓗ Ⓙ   49 Ⓐ Ⓑ Ⓒ Ⓓ Ⓔ

TEST 1.   ENGLISH USAGE

40 Minutes—75 Questions

Directions: In each of the following passages, some portions are underlined and numbered. Corresponding to each numbered portion are three alternative ways of saying the same thing. Read through each passage quickly to determine the sense of the passage, then return to the underlined portions. If you feel that an underlined portion is correct and is stated as well as possible, mark NO CHANGE, A or F. If you feel that there is an error in grammar, sentence structure, punctuation, or word usage, choose the correct answer. If an underlined portion appears to be correct, but you believe that one of the alternative choices would be more effective, mark that choice. Remember, you are to choose the *best* answer.

Passage I

Everyone has at one time or another felt the need to

          1

express himself. What must you do in order to learn to

     2   3

say exactly what you want to say. You will have to

         4   5   6

1. **A.** NO CHANGE
   B. the other
   C. an other
   D. one other

2. **F.** NO CHANGE
   G. theirself
   H. themself
   J. theirselves

3. **A.** NO CHANGE
   B. they
   C. he
   D. one

4. **F.** NO CHANGE
   G. we want
   H. one wants
   J. everyone wants

5. **A.** NO CHANGE
   B. say?
   C. say!
   D. say:

6. **F.** NO CHANGE
   G. They ought to
   H. We should
   J. One must

study <u>very careful</u> the English language and especially
7

7.   **A.** NO CHANGE
      B. with care
      C. carefully (inserted after language)
      D. OMIT

<u>it's</u> <u>grammar—some</u> people think that <u>Good English</u> is
  8   9   10

8.   **F.** NO CHANGE
      G. its
      H. its'
      J. their

9.   **A.** NO CHANGE
      B. grammar. Some
      C. grammar. (begin a new paragraph with Some)
      D. grammar." (begin a new paragraph with Some)

10.   **F.** NO CHANGE
      G. good english
      H. good English
      J. English that is good

fancy English, but this contention <u>isnt</u> true. Just because
11

11.   **A.** NO CHANGE
      B. isn't
      C. aint
      D. aren't

a person uses long <u>words it does not mean that</u>
12

12.   **F.** NO CHANGE
      G. words, it does not mean that
      H. words, you don't know that
      J. words, he does not necessarily

<u>he speaks good.</u> The person <u>whom</u> uses simple words
    13   14

13.   **A.** NO CHANGE
      B. he speaks well.
      C. speak correct.
      D. speak well.

14.   **F.** NO CHANGE
      G. who
      H. what
      J. which

and phrases <u>which say</u> exactly what he means is using
15

15.   **A.** NO CHANGE
      B. what say
      C. which says
      D. who say

better English <u>than</u> the individual who shows off with
16

<u>hard-to understand expressions.</u>
17

16. **F.** NO CHANGE
    G. from
    H. then
    J. instead of

17. **A.** NO CHANGE
    B. hard to understand
       expressions.
    C. hard-to-understand
       expressions.
    D. hard-to-understand-
       expressions.

Passage II

I <u>have received</u> your letter informing me that I am
18
now to be charged an extra dollar per month

<u>for not publishing</u> my telephone number. <u>In other words</u>
19   20
you propose to charge me for nonservice.

18. **F.** NO CHANGE
    G. had received
    H. received
    J. am receiving

19. **A.** NO CHANGE
    B. for not having published
    C. for you not listing
    D. for your not listing

20. **F.** NO CHANGE
    G. In other words,
    H. However,
    J. Moreover,

<u>You give as your reason the fact that</u>
21

<u>not publishing my number</u>
22

incurs additional <u>expense requiring</u> special recordkeep-
23

21. **A.** NO CHANGE
    B. The fact is that the reason
       is
    C. You claim that
    D. You say that

22. **F.** NO CHANGE
    G. by not publishing my
       number
    H. when you don't publish
       my number it
    J. an unpublished number

23. **A.** NO CHANGE
    B. expense, requiring
    C. expense, because of re-
       quiring
    D. expense, because of the
       requirement for

ing and the personal handling of requests for these numbers.
                                                          24

It seems obvious that by not publishing my number you get
                            25

several hundred percent less calls to my number
                26   27   28

and it is therefore less costly to your company to service
                29
an unpublished number than the listed kind.

Your charge is an outrage and your reasoning is an
                        30

insult to normal intelligence but I am forced to pay
                    31

since there is no other outfit I can take my business to.
                                                    32

Its a cheap and shabby bit of stealing by a company that
33

24. F. NO CHANGE
    G. for my number.
    H. for it.
    J. such a number.

25. A. NO CHANGE
    B. an unpublished number receives
    C. when you don't publish my number you get
    D. if you do not publish my number you will not get

26. F. NO CHANGE
    G. hundred %
    H. hundred per centum
    J. hundred per-cent

27. A. NO CHANGE
    B. smaller calls
    C. fewer calls
    D. lesser calls

28. F. NO CHANGE
    G. to it
    H. to that number
    J. OMIT

29. A. NO CHANGE
    B. , and it is therefore
    C. and, it is therefore
    D. and, it is, therefore

30. F. NO CHANGE
    G. outrage! and
    H. outrage, and
    J. outrage; and

31. A. NO CHANGE
    B. intelligence! But
    C. intelligence, But
    D. intelligence; but

32. F. NO CHANGE
    G. I can bring my business to.
    H. I can give my orders to.
    J. to which I can give my business.

33. A. NO CHANGE
    B. It's
    C. This is
    D. The charge is

has been getting away with murder for as many years as
     34   35

we have an anti-trust law in this country. Yet, less you
  36   37

get the impression that we the consumer are completely
                            38

helpless against such exploitation I hereby inform
                            39
you that I intend to bring this matter up

with the civil service commission. I am sure they have
           40   41
a grievance committee to hear complaints

against this sort of thing.
    42

34. **F.** NO CHANGE
    G. has got
    H. got
    J. gets

35. **A.** NO CHANGE
    B. ever since
    C. even though
    D. because

36. **F.** NO CHANGE
    G. we had
    H. we have had
    J. we had had

37. **A.** NO CHANGE
    B. lest
    C. least
    D. unless

38. **F.** NO CHANGE
    G. we, the consumer,
    H. us consumers
    J. we consumers

39. **A.** NO CHANGE
    B. exploitation,
    C. exploitations
    D. exploitations,

40. **F.** NO CHANGE
    G. at the Civil Service Commission.
    H. to the Civil Service Commission.
    J. with the Better Business Bureau.

41. **A.** NO CHANGE
    B. there is
    C. that it has
    D. that there are

42. **F.** NO CHANGE
    G. about this sort of thing.
    H. against unfair practice.
    J. about unfair practices.

Passage III

Do you know <u>its not necessary</u> <u>to always travel</u> to
     43   44

distant lands to <u>bring back</u> things of scientific <u>value?</u>
  45   46   47

Right here in the good old <u>U.S.A.</u> you can find
                            48

hidden treasures. Not every inch of space in <u>our's</u>
                                              49

<u>country have been explored,</u> <u>there are</u> some spots still un-
50   51

<u>known to American's.</u>
          52

43. **A.** NO CHANGE
    B. that its not
    C. that it is'nt
    D. that it isn't

44. **F.** NO CHANGE
    G. to travel
    H. to travel always
    J. to always go traveling

45. **A.** NO CHANGE
    B. lands of great distance
    C. distant land's
    D. distance lands

46. **F.** NO CHANGE
    G. take back
    H. bring
    J. take

47. **A.** NO CHANGE
    B. values?
    C. valuability?
    D. valuableness?

48. **F.** NO CHANGE
    G. U.S. of A.
    H. US
    J. United states of America

49. **A.** NO CHANGE
    B. ours
    C. ours'
    D. our

50. **F.** NO CHANGE
    G. countries have
    H. countries has
    J. country has

51. **A.** NO CHANGE
    B. explored; there
    C. explored, they're
    D. explored; they're

52. **F.** NO CHANGE
    G. Americans.
    H. Americans!
    J. American citizens.

Consider the Atlantic seaboard
‾‾‾‾‾‾   ‾‾‾‾‾‾‾‾‾‾‾‾‾‾‾
  53   54

and the Mississippi valley, where there are beautiful
        ‾‾‾‾‾‾‾‾‾‾‾‾‾‾‾‾
              55

wild-birds never captured by man.
‾‾‾‾‾‾‾‾ ‾‾‾‾‾
  56   57

Passage IV

It was lack of power and speed that once again brings
                                                ‾‾‾‾‾
                                                 58

about the Yankees' defeat. They couldn't run fast
‾‾‾‾‾   ‾‾‾‾‾‾‾‾‾‾‾‾‾
          59

enough to break up the Ranger's double plays; and
                       ‾‾‾‾‾‾‾‾‾‾‾‾‾‾‾‾‾‾‾‾‾
                                60
in the field they were unable to get to drives that

in the past years would have been turned into outs.
                      ‾‾‾‾‾‾‾‾‾‾‾‾‾‾‾‾‾‾‾‾‾‾‾‾
                                61

The flashy style of Buddy Bell at third, making
‾‾‾‾‾‾‾‾‾‾‾‾‾‾‾‾‾‾‾‾‾‾‾‾‾‾‾‾‾‾‾‾‾‾‾‾‾‾‾
              62

53. A. NO CHANGE
    B. For example,
    C. In some areas of
    D. Along

54. F. NO CHANGE
    G. Atlantic-seaboard
    H. Atlantic-seabored
    J. Atlantic Seaboard

55. A. NO CHANGE
    B. Mississippi-valley
    C. Mississippi Valley
    D. Mississippi's valley

56. F. NO CHANGE
    G. wildbirds
    H. Wildbirds
    J. wild birds

57. A. NO CHANGE
    B. never before captured
    C. never even seen
    D. never, captured

58. F. NO CHANGE
    G. bring
    H. brung
    J. brought

59. A. NO CHANGE
    B. Yankee's defeat.
    C. Yankees defeat!
    D. Yankees' defeat!

60. F. NO CHANGE
    G. Rangers' double-plays
    H. Rangers' double plays,
    J. Ranger's double plays

61. A. NO CHANGE
    B. have been turned out.
    C. have been out.
    D. have been certain outs.

62. F. NO CHANGE
    G. The flashy third baseman Buddy Bell
    H. Buddy Bell's flashy style at third
    J. Buddy Bell's flash and style at third

plays as clean as though he is using a broom, was only a
_____ _____ _____
63   64   65
part of the Rangers' play. They came on strong and

63. A. NO CHANGE
    B. plays, cleanly
    C. plays as cleanly
    D. plays, as cleanly

64. F. NO CHANGE
    G. as if
    H. like as if
    J. like as though

65. A. NO CHANGE
    B. uses
    C. has used
    D. were using

were as hard to catch as the lawmen for whom they
                                        66
were named. Each time the Yankees threatened to

66. F. NO CHANGE
    G. for who
    H. for what
    J. for which

score, the Rangers came up with the big play. And when
                                        67
a man like Jackson of the Yankees strikes out three

67. A. NO CHANGE
    B. When
    C. And if
    D. If

times you can figure upon the strength of Ranger
              68
pitching. Jackson is one of the game's best hitters, but

68. F. NO CHANGE
    G. sort of figure
    H. estimate
    J. be sure of

yesterday finding nothing that he could touch.
          69

69. A. NO CHANGE
    B. he has found
    C. he found
    D. he founded

A strong point in the Yankee teams' favor was its
                                       70
refusal to give up even when the Rangers were well on

70. F. NO CHANGE
    G. it's
    H. there
    J. their

there way to a third straight victory.
71

71. A. NO CHANGE
    B. their
    C. our
    D. its

New York is a better team than it had last year. So
                                          72
has Texas. We doubt, though, that any team in the
American League could have beaten the Rangers

72. F. NO CHANGE
    G. are
    H. was
    J. has

yesterday afternoon—<u>Eastern or Western Division.</u>
73

73. **A.** NO CHANGE
B. (place this after League, set off by dashes)
C. (place this after team, set off by commas)
D. (place this after Tigers, set off within parentheses)

The Yankee team <u>hasn't no</u> cause for despair over
74

74. **F.** NO CHANGE
G. have no
H. has no
J. hasn't got any

<u>its showing</u> against those odds.
75

75. **A.** NO CHANGE
B. its showing,
C. it's showing
D. it's showing,

END OF TEST

If you complete this test before the time is up, look back over the questions. Do not proceed to the next test until you are told to do so.

yesterday afternoon—Eastern or Western Division.
                            ‾‾‾‾‾‾‾‾‾‾‾‾‾‾‾‾‾‾‾‾‾‾‾‾‾‾
                                        73

73. **A.** NO CHANGE
      B. (place this after League, set off by dashes)
      C. (place this after team, set off by commas)
      D. (place this after Tigers, set off within parentheses)

The Yankee team hasn't no cause for despair over
                  ‾‾‾‾‾‾‾‾‾‾
                       74

74. **F.** NO CHANGE
      G. have no
      H. has no
      J. hasn't got any

its showing against those odds.
‾‾‾‾‾‾‾‾‾
   75

75. **A.** NO CHANGE
      B. its showing,
      C. it's showing
      D. it's showing,

END OF TEST

If you complete this test before the time is up, look back over the questions. Do not proceed to the next test until you are told to do so.

TEST 2. MATHEMATICS USAGE

50 Minutes—40 Questions

Directions: Solve each problem and mark the letter of the correct
answer on your answer sheet.

1. What is 40% of $\frac{10}{7}$?

   A. $\frac{2}{7}$

   B. $\frac{4}{7}$

   C. $\frac{10}{28}$

   D. $\frac{1}{28}$

   E. $\frac{28}{10}$

2. A prime number is one which is divisible only by itself and 1. Which of
   the following are prime numbers?
   I. 17
   II. 27
   III. 51
   IV. 59

   F. I only
   G. I and II only
   H. I, III, and IV only
   J. I and IV only
   K. III and IV only

3. As shown in the diagram, AB is a straight line and angle BOC = 20°.
   If the number of degrees in angle DOC is 6 more than the number of
   degrees in angle x, find the number of degrees in angle x.

   A. 77°
   B. 75°
   C. 78°
   D. $22\frac{6}{7}$°
   E. 87°

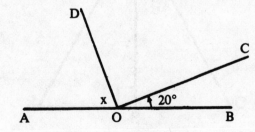

4. As shown in the figure below, a cylindrical oil tank is one-third full. If 3 more gallons are added, the tank will be one-half full. What is the capacity, in gallons, of the tank?

   F. 15 gallons
   G. 16 gallons
   H. 17 gallons
   J. 18 gallons
   K. 19 gallons

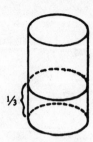

5. A girl receives grades of 91, 88, 86, and 78 in four of her major subjects. What must she receive in her fifth major subject in order to average 85?

   A. 86
   B. 85
   C. 84
   D. 83
   E. 82

6. If a steel bar is 0.39 feet long, its length in inches is

   F. less than 4

   G. between 4 and $4\frac{1}{2}$

   H. between $4\frac{1}{2}$ and 5

   J. between 5 and 6
   K. more than 6

7. In the figure, PS is perpendicular to QR. If PQ = PR = 26 and PS = 24, then QR =

   A. 14
   B. 16
   C. 18
   D. 20
   E. 22

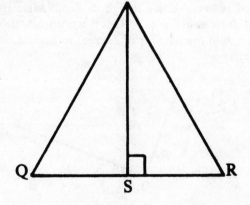

8. If x = 0, for what value of y is the equation $5x^3 + 7x^2 - (4y + 13)x - 7y + 15 = 0$ valid?

   F. $-2\frac{1}{7}$

   G. 0

   H. $2\frac{1}{7}$

   J. $\frac{15}{11}$

   K. $3\frac{1}{7}$

9. A woman spends exactly $81 buying some shirts and string ties. If the shirts cost $7 and the string ties cost $3 each, what is the ratio of shirts to string ties purchased when more shirts than ties are purchased?

   A. 5:3
   B. 4:3
   C. 5:2
   D. 4:1
   E. 3:2

10. If a woman walks $\frac{2}{5}$ mile in 5 minutes, what is her average rate of walking in miles per hour?

    F. 4 m.p.h.

    G. $4\frac{1}{2}$ m.p.h.

    H. $4\frac{4}{5}$ m.p.h.

    J. $5\frac{1}{5}$ m.p.h.

    K. $5\frac{3}{4}$ m.p.h.

11. One end of a dam has the shape of a trapezoid with the dimensions indicated. What is the dam's area in square feet?

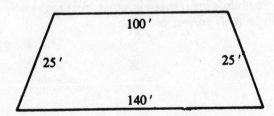

    A. 1000
    B. 1200
    C. 1500
    D. 1800
    E. cannot be determined from the information given

12. If $1 + \dfrac{1}{t} = \dfrac{t+1}{t}$, what does t equal?

    F. + 2 only
    G. + 2 or − 2 only
    H. + 2 or −1 only
    J. − 2 or + 1 only
    K. t is any number except 0.

13. Point A is 3 inches from line b as shown in the diagram. In the plane that contains point A and line b, what is the total number of points which are 6 inches from A and also 1 inch from b?

    A. 0
    B. 1
    C. 2
    D. 3
    E. 4

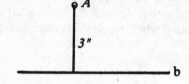

14. If R and S are different integers both divisible by 5, then which of the following is *not necessarily* true?

    F. R − S is divisible by 5
    G. RS is divisible by 25
    H. R + S is divisible by 5
    J. $R^2 + S^2$ is divisible by 5
    K. R + S is divisible by 10

15. If a triangle of base 7 is equal in area to a circle of radius 7, what is the altitude of the triangle?

    A. 8π
    B. 10π
    C. 12π
    D. 14π
    E. cannot be determined from the information given

16. If the following numbers are arranged in order from the smallest to the largest, what will be their correct order?

    I. $\dfrac{9}{13}$

    II. $\dfrac{13}{9}$

    III. 70%

    IV. $\dfrac{1}{.70}$

    F. II, I, III, IV
    G. III, II, I, IV
    H. III, IV, I, II
    J. II, IV, III, I
    K. I, III, IV, II

17. The coordinates of the vertices of quadrilateral PQRS are P (0, 0), Q (9, 0), R (10, 3), and S (1, 3) respectively. The area of PQRS is

    A. $9\sqrt{10}$

    B. $\frac{9}{2}\sqrt{10}$

    C. $\frac{27}{2}$

    D. 27

    E. cannot be determined from the information given

18. In the circle shown, AB is a diameter. If secant AP = 8 and tangent CP = 4, find the number of units in the diameter of the circle.

    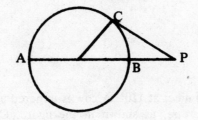

    F. 6

    G. $6\frac{1}{2}$

    H. 8

    J. $3\sqrt{2}$

    K. cannot be determined from the information given

19. A certain type of siding for a house costs $10.50 per square yard. What does it cost for the siding of a wall 4 yards wide and 60 feet long?

    A. $800

    B. $840

    C. $2520

    D. $3240

    E. $5040

20. A circle whose radius is 7 has its center at the origin. Which of the following points are outside the circle?

    I. (4, 4)

    II. (5, 5)

    III. (4, 5)

    IV. (4, 6)

    F. I and II only

    G. II and III only

    H. II, III, and IV only

    J. II and IV only

    K. III and IV only

21. A merchant sells a radio for $80, thereby making a profit of 25% of the cost. What is the ratio of cost to selling price?

    A. $\frac{4}{5}$

    B. $\frac{3}{4}$

    C. $\frac{5}{6}$

    D. $\frac{2}{3}$

    E. $\frac{3}{5}$

22. How many degrees are between the hands of a clock at 3:40?

    F. 150°
    G. 140°
    H. 130°
    J. 125°
    K. 120°

23. Two fences in a field meet at 120°. A cow is tethered at their intersection with a 15-foot rope, as shown in the figure. Over how many square feet may the cow graze?

    A. 50π
    B. 75π
    C. 80π
    D. 85π
    E. 90π

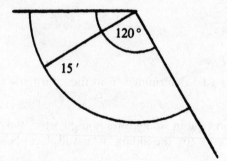

24. If $\frac{17}{10}y = 0.51$, then y =

    F. 3
    G. 1.3
    H. 1.2
    J. .3
    K. .03

25. A junior class of 50 girls and 70 boys sponsored a dance. If 40% of the girls and 50% of the boys attended the dance, approximately what percent of the class attended?

    A. 40%
    B. 42%
    C. 44%
    D. 46%
    E. 48%

26. In the figure below, *r*, *s*, and *t* are straight lines meeting at point p, with angles formed as indicated; y=

F. 30°
G. 120°
H. 3x
J. 180 − x
K. 180 − 3x

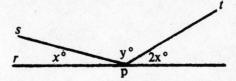

27. $\dfrac{18}{33} = \dfrac{\sqrt{36}}{\sqrt{?}}$

A. 11
B. 121
C. 66
D. 144
E. 1089

28. If we write all the whole numbers from 200 to 400, how many of these contain the digit 7 once and only once?

F. 32
G. 34
H. 35
J. 36
K. 38

29. $(r + s)^2 - r^2 - s^2 = (?)$

A. 2rs
B. rs
C. rs^2
D. 0
E. $2r^2 + 2s^2$

30. In the figure below, angle S is obtuse, PR = 9, PS = 6, and Q is any point on RS. Which of the following inequalities expresses possible values of the length of PQ?

F. 9 ⩾ PQ ⩾ 6
G. 9 ⩾ 6 ⩾ PQ
H. 6 ⩾ PQ ⩾ 9
J. PQ ⩾ 9 ⩾ 6
K. 9 ⩽ PQ ⩽ 6

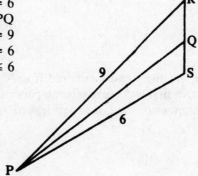

31. If a woman buys several articles for K cents per dozen and sells them for $\frac{K}{8}$ cents per article, what is her profit, in cents, per article?

A. $\frac{K}{48}$

B. $\frac{K}{12}$

C. $\frac{3K}{4}$

D. $\frac{K}{18}$

E. $\frac{K}{24}$

32. If all P are S and no S are Q, it necessarily follows that

F. all Q are S
G. all Q are P
H. no P are Q
J. no S are P
K. some Q are P

33. The average of four numbers is 45. If one of the numbers is increased by 6, the average will remain unchanged if each of the other three numbers is reduced by

A. 1
B. 2
C. $\frac{3}{4}$
D. 4
E. $\frac{4}{3}$

34. Given the series 3, 12, 21, 30, 39, 48 . . . , which of the following will be a member of this series?

F. 10,000
G. 10,002
H. 9999
J. 101,000
K. none of these

35. A set of papers is arranged and numbered from 1 to 40. If the paper numbered 4 is drawn first and every seventh paper thereafter is drawn, what will be the number of the last paper drawn?

A. 36
B. 37
C. 38
D. 39
E. 40

36. If the angles of a triangle are in the ratio of 2:3:5, the triangle is

    F. obtuse
    G. acute
    H. isosceles
    J. right
    K. equilateral

37. In the figure, a rectangular piece of cardboard 18 inches by 24 inches is made into an open box by cutting a 5-inch square from each corner and building up the sides. What is the volume of the box in cubic inches?

    A. 560 cubic inches
    B. 1233 cubic inches
    C. 1560 cubic inches
    D. 2160 cubic inches
    E. 4320 cubic inches

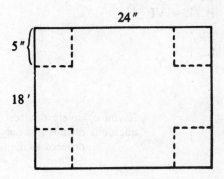

38. The figure below represents the back of a house. Find, in feet, the length of one of the equal rafters, PQ or QR, if each extends 12 inches beyond the eaves.

    F. 19 feet
    G. 21 feet
    H. 23 feet
    J. 25 feet
    K. 43 feet

39. The scale of a certain map is $\frac{3}{4}$ inch = 9 miles. Find in square miles the actual area of a park represented on the map by a square whose side is $\frac{7}{8}$ inch.

    A. $10\frac{1}{2}$ square miles

   B. 21 square miles

   C. $110\frac{1}{4}$ square miles

   D. 121 square miles

   E. $125\frac{2}{3}$ square miles

40. A relationship that holds for all waves is expressed by the formula V = fL, where V is the velocity, f is the frequency, and L is the wavelength. Express the wavelength L in terms of V and f.

   F. $L = \dfrac{V}{f}$

   G. $L = V - f$

   H. $L = Vf$

   J. $L = V + f$

   K. $L = \dfrac{f}{V}$

END OF TEST

If you complete this test before the time is up, check back over the questions on this test only. Do not return to the previous test. Do not proceed to the next test until you are told to do so.

TEST 3.   SOCIAL STUDIES READING

35 Minutes—52 Questions

Directions: Below each of the following reading passages is a series of questions. Choose the *best* answer to each question, interpreting what is stated or implied by the passage in the light of your own background in the subject. You may refer back to the passage as often as necessary, though the answers to some questions may not be found expressly in the passage.

Although most high school students lead active lives through involvement in extracurricular activities, many students, especially girls, spend much time watching soap operas.

Regular soap operas viewers watch soaps anywhere from one to five times per week. Although the reasons why *soapoperatics* watch soaps differ, most viewers agree that they "get hooked on them." One disparager of this trend suggests that watching soap operas is addictive, somewhat like using drugs; it dulls the mind and becomes habit-forming.

Supporting this claim, one student who regularly watches "General Hospital," the most popular soap, explains that she watches because she "must see what is happening to Laura and Scotty," two of the program's characters.

Other students are attracted to soap operas for emotional reasons. Many find the soaps "hysterical" or "ridiculous." A sophomore boy devotee watches "General Hospital" daily because "I love to see people with so many problems!"

Still other students, mainly girls, claim that they watch soap operas because the soaps provide a source for conversation with peers. As one girl puts it, "It isn't nice to gossip about people you know, but it is socially acceptable to talk about the characters in the soaps." A disgusted boy comments, "All you hear girls talking about nowadays are soap operas—they watch all of them."

Some students watch soaps to "pass the time," especially while they babysit. Others agree with the senior who refuses to watch soaps because they are "inane, stupid, and a waste of time." While many soap opera viewers are attracted by the element of pathos in soaps, nonviewers may be repelled by this same aspect. One nonviewer says that soaps are too "emotional," while another, who hates suspense, says, "They drive me up the wall."

Still, many students obviously watch soaps. In a paper on the good and evil effects of wealth, reports an English teacher, students used more examples from soap operas than from literature. This teacher regards the viewing of soaps as a "fashion that spreads like a new style of clothing," which acts as a "pollutant of the intellectual environment."

Speaking of the effects of soap opera viewing on students, the English teacher asserts, "It makes their brains soggy—the soap opera doesn't challenge their thinking." The teacher also views this "indulgence" as a waste of time. He agrees that we all need occasional retreats from routine and responsibility, but suggests that a carefully planned regimen of intellectual exercise is sometimes better than this type of indulgence.

Adapted from an article in the Scarsdale High School *Maroon*, with permission of the editor.

1. The writer of this article is

   A. objective
   B. approving
   C. judgmental
   D. disapproving

2. The phenomenon of soap opera addiction should be of scientific interest to
   I. psychologists
   II. sociologists
   III. English teachers
   IV. historians

   F. I only
   G. I and II
   G. I, II, and III
   J. I, II, III, and IV

3. Addiction to soap operas among teenagers is mostly

   A. an emotional outlet
   B. a social outlet
   C. an intellectual exercise
   D. a new fad

4. An example of rationalization in this article is the statement

   F. "I love to see people with so many problems!"
   G. "It isn't nice to gossip about people you know, but it is socially acceptable to talk about the characters in the soaps."
   H. "All you hear girls talking about nowadays are soap operas—they watch all of them."
   J. ". . . students used more examples from soap operas than from literature."

5. If one could claim that watching soaps is governed by an *instinct*, that *instinct* would be

   A. inertia—the instinctive need to sit and do nothing
   B. sexual—sublimation of this instinct into vicarious stimulation through the soap opera characters
   C. social—the instinct to conform and to belong to the *in group*
   D. mental stimulation—the instinctive need to have something to think about

6. Objections to habitual watching of soap operas include the
   I. narcotic effect on the mind
   II. heavy emotional content
   III. time wasted
   IV. gossip engendered

   F. I and III
   G. II and IV
   H. I, II, and IV
   J. I, II, and III

7. Soap operas are so named because

   A. they serve as emotional catharsis or cleansing
   B. the situations portrayed are contrived and "frothy"
   C. they were once watched mainly by housewives as a respite from cleaning house
   D. they are traditionally sponsored by soap companies

8. The English teacher feels that

   F. it is good that students are able to use examples from soap operas in their written work
   G. studying the soaps is a good intellectual exercise
   H. there are better forms of recreation
   J. the latest fads in clothing are disgraceful

"Each State shall appoint, in such Manner as the Legislature thereof may direct, a Number of Electors, equal to the whole Number of Senators and Representatives to which the State may be entitled in the Congress; but no Senator or Representative, or Person holding an Office of Trust or Profit under the United States, shall be appointed an Elector.

"The Electors shall meet in their respective States, and vote by Ballot for two Persons, of whom one at least shall not be an inhabitant of the same State with themselves. And they shall make a List of all the Persons voted for, and of the

Number of Votes for each; which List they shall sign and certify, and transmit sealed to the Seat of the Government of the United States, directed to the President of the Senate. The President of the Senate shall, in the Presence of the Senate and House of Representatives, open all the Certificates, and the Votes shall then be counted. The Person having the greatest Number of Votes shall be the President, if such Number be a Majority of the whole Number of Electors appointed; and if there be more than one who have such Majority, and have an equal Number of Votes, then the House of Representatives shall immediately chuse by Ballot one of them for President; and if no person have a Majority, then from the five highest on the List the said House shall in like manner chuse the President. But in chusing the President, the Votes shall be taken by States, the Representation from each State having one Vote; A quorum for this Purpose shall consist of a Member or Members from two thirds of the States, and a Majority of the States shall be necessary to a Choice. In every Case, after the Choice of President, the Person having the greatest Number of Votes of the Electors shall be the Vice President. But if there should remain two or more who have equal Votes, the Senate shall chuse from them by Ballot the Vice President.

"The Congress may determine the Time of chusing the Electors, and the Day on which they shall give their Votes; which Day shall be the same throughout the United States."

9. The people who actually elect the President are known as the

A. electorate
B. Congress
C. majority
D. electors

10. If a state has 27 members in the House of Representatives, its total number of electoral votes would be

F. 27
G. 29
H. 54
J. dependent on the number of people who voted in the state

11. The person responsible for opening the electoral ballots is the

A. President of the Congress
B. Vice President of the United States
C. majority leader of the House
D. Chairman of the election committee

12. Of the following, which one could qualify as an elector?

F. A United States Senator
G. The Secretary of State of the U.S.
H. The Governor of N.Y. State
J. The Vice President of the U.S.

13. If a presidential candidate receives 45 percent of the popular vote

A. he cannot become the next President
B. he may still win the election
C. he will receive 45 percent of the electoral vote
D. his election would be dependent on the Senate

14. The votes of the electors must be sent to

F. Washington, D.C.
G. the state capitols
H. the headquarters of the leading candidates
J. the Republican and Democratic party chairpeople

15. People who consider this plan "undemocratic" would rather see the President elected by

A. the electoral college
B. Congress
C. popular vote
D. written ballot

16. According to the electoral system, the number of people who may be nominated to become President

F. allows for only a two-party system
G. is limited to three people

H. is limited to the candidates of majority parties

J. is not limited to a set number

17. At no time in the history of the United States have we had a President and a Vice President from the same state. This is because

    A. talent is naturally geographically distributed, so the best-qualified persons are never from the same state

    B. the nominating conventions hope that people will vote for a candidate from their own state; therefore they nominate candidates from more than one state

    C. it is unconstitutional for both President and Vice President to come from the same state

    D. some electors would be disenfranchised if presidential and vice-presidential candidates were from the same state

18. The document quoted here is, of course, the United States Constitution (Article II, Section 1). The Twelfth Amendment has altered the prescribed method for choosing the Vice President. The purpose of the change was to

    F. allow the President to choose his own Vice President

    G. permit voting for a "ticket"

    H. avoid the too likely possibility that the President and Vice President might be of opposing parties and politically incompatible

    J. allow the Vice President to come from the same state as the President

19. The framers of the Constitution were intelligent men with great vision, but their education left them poorly prepared in
     I. spelling
    II. capitalization and punctuation
    III. mathematics

    A. none of these
    B. I and II
    C. III
    D. I, II, and III

20. According to the Constitution, if the electors fail to elect a President, the House of Representatives must do so

    F. at the time the ballots are counted
    G. on a date set by mutual agreement of both houses
    H. by March 4
    J. by January 20

21. The electoral collge is

    A. in Washington, D.C.
    B. a creation of the press
    C. a fictional body
    D. a semantic term

22. The Constitution provides that the electors be

    F. appointed by the legislature of each state
    G. appointed by the congressional delegation of each state
    H. elected by the people of each state
    J. appointed according to the directions of each state legislature

SPEAKER NUMBER ONE

Many schemes have been devised to strengthen our economy and raise our standard of living. The irony of the situation is that nothing needs to be done. The best method of improving our economy is to rely on human instinct: on the ability of people to pay to have their own wants satisfied and to profit from satisfying the wants of others. The Constitution guarantees the pursuit of happiness, but many of the collectivist schemes try to guarantee happiness itself by the use of handouts. We do not need a super-government dictating what both management and labor need to do to be productive.

If we go back to the old fashioned competition upon which the country has prospered we will find that the cost of government will drop and we can lower taxes. This will increase the amount of money available for investment and production. The increase in activity is what our economy needs to prosper and give all our people a chance to strive for happiness.

SPEAKER NUMBER TWO

We all agree that it is important to improve our economy and to end the social and economic crises resulting from a faltering economy. Past experience has shown that unless definite controls are placed upon concentrations of economic power the economy will not properly regulate itself. We must not allow monopolies to destroy the freedom of the marketplace. We must protect the purchasing power of our senior citizens through continuation of social security programs. We most control the flow of currency through the use of a graduated income tax. In short, we must use those tools which the science of economics has developed to control our own economy. Only in that way will everyone be able to share in its growth.

23. What is the most basic difference between the two points of view presented here?

A. whether or not our economy should be made stronger
B. how much government control should be used in our economic system
C. whether or not we should have competition in our economy
D. the place of democracy in our economic system

24. How would Speaker Number One feel about strengthening the Sherman Anti-Trust Act? The speaker would

F. like it because it strengthens competition
G. agree only if it proved to be constitutional
H. oppose it as unnecessary government intereference
J. oppose it because he feels it is undemocratic

25. How would Speaker Number One feel about strikes which bring industry to a halt?

A. The speaker would want them settled through government-sponsored mediation.
B. The speaker would feel strikes should not be allowed if they interrupt our economy.
C. Strikes are a natural way for differences to be worked out between labor and management.
D. Strikes are the result of large companies' refusing to treat their workers fairly.

26. Which of the following taxes would Speaker Number Two most likely oppose? A (An)

F. Corporate Tax
G. Inheritance Tax
H. Income Tax
J. Sales Tax

27. "The more complex our economy becomes, the more necessary government controls become." Which speaker would agree with this statement?

A. Both speakers would agree.
B. Neither speaker would agree.
C. Only Speaker Number One would agree.
D. Only Speaker Number Two would agree.

28. The philosophy espoused by Speaker Number One is

F. laissez-faire
G. protectionism
H. patriotism
J. democracy

29. "Ups and downs in business cycles are not desirable." Which speaker would agree with this statement?

A. Both speakers would agree.
B. Neither speaker would agree.
C. Only Speaker Number One would agree.
D. Only Speaker Number Two would agree.

30. On the basis of the stated views, we may assume that Speaker Number One would be opposed to the
  I. OSHA
  II. CIA
  III. FHA
  IV. FDIC

  F. I and III
  G. II and IV
  H. I, III, and IV
  J. none of these

31. On the basis of the stated views, we may assume that Speaker Number Two would be opposed to the
  I. OSHA
  II. CIA
  II. FHA
  IV. FDIC

  A. I and III
  B. II and IV
  C. I, III, and IV
  D. none of these

Directions: Questions 32–44 are not based on a reading passage. Choose the *best* answer to each question in accordance with your background and understanding in social studies.

32. The Northwest Ordinance of 1787 provided for the

  F. admission of new states to the Union as equals of the original states
  G. admission of new states to the Union with popular sovereignty on slavery
  H. creation of self-governing territories independent of Congress
  J. creation of new states governed by Congressional Committees

33. The 3/5 Compromise at the Constitutional Convention of 1787 provided that

  A. for purposes of representation and taxation, the votes of three free men were equal to those of five slaves
  B. for purposes of representation and taxation, five slaves would be counted as three free persons
  C. the votes of 3/5 of the slave-holding states would be needed to pass any legislation affecting slavery
  D. the votes of 3/5 of the southern states would be needed to pass any legislation affecting representation or taxation

34. One reason why the United States declared war on England rather than on France in 1812 was that

  F. Napoleon had respected American rights as neutrals
  G. New England shipowners and merchants had clamored for war with England

  H. western expansionists in Congress wished to annex Canada
  J. the French had great naval power in the Caribbean

35. The following problems were all common to the post-war settlements of both World War I and World War II *except*

  A. the Italo-Yugoslav boundary
  B. the Polish boundaries
  C. Russian intransigence at post-war conferences
  D. reparations from the defeated countries

36. Of the following, which one constitutes an implicit cost to a firm?

  F. payments made on leased equipment
  G. taxes paid to a local municipality for real estate
  H. salaries paid to its legal consultants
  J. depreciation of company-owned equipment

37. Most members of delinquent juvenile gangs are

  A. mentally retarded
  B. psychopaths
  C. paranoid
  D. normal except for their delinquency

38. The independent territory of Texas was annexed in 1845 by

    F. executive order
    G. a joint resolution of Congress
    H. a formal treaty between the United States and Texas
    J. the Treaty of Guadalupe Hidalgo

39. Which of the following statements most accurately describes Union policy toward black troops?

    A. Former slaves were not permitted to serve in the Union Army.
    B. Former slaves were allowed to join the Union Army but were not permitted to become officers.
    C. The 13th Amendment guaranteed blacks admission into the Union Army.
    D. One hundred seventy thousand black troops served in the Union Army after the first combat year.

40. Immigrants in the late nineteenth century established their own self-help organizations in the form of

    F. settlement houses
    G. political parties
    H. burial and insurance societies
    J. public schools

41. The Supreme Court decided that separate facilities for blacks were legally equal to those provided for whites in

    A. *Brown* v. *Board of Education*
    B. *Muller* v. *Oregon*
    C. *Plessy* v. *Ferguson*
    D. *Gibbons* v. *Ogden*

42. Which one of the following was *not* a cause of controversy between the United States and England in the period immediately following the Treaty of Paris of 1783?

    F. debts owed to English merchants
    G. the impressment of American seamen
    H. the treatment of Loyalists
    J. the northern boundary of the new nation

43. Which one of the following was *not* a cause for rivalry between England and the Netherlands in the seventeenth century?

    A. competition for fisheries in the North Sea
    B. rivalry for commercial posts in the East Indies
    C. control of settlements in America
    D. antagonism arising from religious differences

44. The League of Nations was established in 1919 by

    F. the "Fourteen Points"
    G. a joint vote of Congress
    H. the Versailles Treaty
    J. the recommendation of the Senate Foreign Relations Commitee

The development of voting laws in England is important to us because they were the basis of voting laws in colonial America. As England began to change from an agricultural country to an industrial country, the absolute power of the King began to dissolve. Those who began to have economic power also began to have political power. This political power was recognized by the English "Bill of Rights" passed in 1689. In order that this power would not become further diluted, early English voting laws were based on requirements of land ownership and formal education.

While these same restrictions were followed in colonial America, the effect was different. In England the poor could not own land, but in America land could be acquired by simply clearing and working it. This new political power, coupled with independent economic power, resulted in a new kind of democracy which eventually led to the Declaration of Independence and the U.S. Constitution.

45. The main purpose of this article is to

A. describe the parliamentary law of 1689
B. show why voting laws are necessary
C. explain the voting laws of England
D. explain the background of voting laws in America

46. What does the author cite as an important factor in the changes in voting laws?

F. changes in economic situations
G. colonization
H. modern ideas of government
J. the growth of world population

47. Which one of the following is the best example of the economic power mentioned in this article? The ability to

A. buy land
B. pay the costs of government
C. bribe public officials
D. buy votes

48. Judging from this passage, which one of the following qualifications probably became the most important factor in voting as a result of the 1689 "Bill of Rights"?

F. religion
G. money
H. education
J. ancestry

49. The first people allowed to vote in England probably gained this right as the result of

A. religion
B. money
C. education
D. ancestry

50. The purpose of the "Bill of Rights" of 1689 was to

F. furnish a pattern for colonial America
G. outlaw tyranny of any kind
H. guard the voting rights of all citizens
J. formalize the sharing of political power

51. What would be the most likely reason for the King of England's signing of the 1689 "Bill of Rights?" He

A. received a great deal of money for doing so
B. was forced to sign in order to retain his position
C. wanted to share his responsibilities
D. felt democracy was the best form of government

52. The United States Bill of Rights

F. is patterned closely on the English "Bill of Rights"
G. was passed shortly after the English "Bill of Rights"
H. completely rejects the English "Bill of Rights"
J. is unrelated to the English "Bill of Rights"

END OF TEST

If you complete this test before the time is up, check back over the questions on this test only. Do not go back to any previous tests. Do not proceed to the next test until you are told to do so.

TEST 4.   NATURAL SCIENCE READING

35 Minutes—52 Questions

Directions: Below each of the following reading passages is a series of questions. Choose the *best* answer to each question, interpreting what is stated or implied by the passage in the light of your own background in the subject. You may refer back to the passage as often as necessary, though the answers to some questions may not be found expressly in the passage.

An action of apparent social significance among animals is that of migration. But several different factors are at work causing such migrations. These may be concerned with food-getting; with temperature, salinity, pressure, and light changes; with the action of sex hormones; and probably other combinations of these factors.

The great aggregations of small crustaceans, such as copepods found at the surface of the ocean, swarms of insects about a light, or the masses of unicellular organisms making up a part of the plankton in the lakes and oceans are all examples of nonsocial aggregations of organisms brought together because of the presence or absence of certain factors in their environment, such as air currents, water currents, food or the lack of it, oxygen or carbon dioxide, or some other contributing causes.

Insects make long migrations, most of which seem due to the urge for food. The migrations of the locust, both in this country and elsewhere, are well known. While fish, such as salmon, return to the same stream where they grew up, such return migrations are rare in insects, the only known instance being in the monarch butterfly. This is apparently due to the fact that it is long-lived and has the power of strong flight. The mass migrations of the Rocky Mountain and the African species of locust seem attributable to the need for food. Locusts live, eat, sun themselves, and migrate in groups. It has been suggested that their social life is in response to the two fundamental instincts, aggregation and imitation.

Migrations of fish have been studied carefully by many investigators. Typically, the migrations are from deep to shallow waters, as in the herring, mackerel, and many other marine fish. Freshwater fish in general exhibit this type of migration in the spawning season. Spawning habits of many fish show a change in habitat from salt to fresh water. Among these are the shad, salmon, alewife, and others. In the North American and European eels, long migrations take place at the breeding season. All these migrations are obviously not brought about by a quest for food, for the salmon and many other fish feed only sparingly during the spawning season, but are undoubtedly brought about by metabolic changes in the animal initiated by the interaction of sex hormones. If this thesis holds, then here is the beginning of social life.

Bird migrations have long been a matter of study. The reasons for the migration of the golden plover from the Arctic regions to the tip of South America and return in a single year are not fully explainable. Several theories have been advanced, although none has been fully proved. The reproductive "instinct," food scarcity, temperature and light changes, the metabolic changes brought about by the activity of sex hormones, and the length of the day all have been suggested, and ultimately several may prove to be factors. Aside from other findings, it is interesting to note that bird migrations take place year after year on about the same dates. Recent studies in the biochemistry of metabolism, showing that there is a seasonal cycle in the blood sugar that has a definite relation to activity and food, seem to be among the most promising leads.

In mammals the seasonal migrations that take place, such as those of the deer, which travel from the high mountains in summer to the valleys in the winter, or the migration of the caribou in the northern areas of Canada, are based on the factor of temperature which regulates the food supply. A real mystery is the migration of the lemming, a small ratlike animal found in Scandinavia and Canada. The lemming population varies greatly from year to year, and, at times when it greatly increases, a migration occurs in which hordes of lemmings march across the country, swimming rivers and even plunging into the ocean if it bars their way. This again cannot be a purely social association of animals. The horde is usually made up entirely of males, as the females seldom migrate.

1. The migration of the lemmings cannot be considered as a simple instance of social association since

   A. only males migrate
   B. the migrants do not return
   C. the migration appears to be purposeful
   D. it occurs only when the community appears to be thriving

2. A characteristic of migration is the return of the migrants to their former home areas. This, however, is not true of

   F. birds
   G. insects
   H. mammals
   J. fish

3. The reproductive instinct is probably not a factor in the actual migration of

   A. shad
   B. lemming
   C. golden plover
   D. monarch butterfly

4. In paragraph 1, several probable factors causing migrations are given. None of these seems to explain the migrations of

   F. lemming
   G. caribou
   H. salmon
   J. locusts

5. The reasons for the migrations of birds may ultimately be determined by scientists working in the field of

   A. population studies
   B. ecology
   C. metabolism chemistry
   D. reproduction

6. According to the passage, the reproductive process seems to be the main factor in the migration of many

   F. fish
   G. mammals
   H. insects
   J. birds

7. Animals which migrate back and forth between the same general areas are

   A. locusts and salmon
   B. salmon and golden plover
   C. golden plover and lemming
   D. monarch butterfly and honey bee

8. One-way migrations are usually associated with animals that

   F. make long migrations
   G. are long-lived
   H. have short lives
   J. make short migrations

9. The main purpose of the passage is to

   A. show how a natural event effects change in different species
   B. present a new theory in regard to biological evolution
   C. describe a phenomenon that has not yet been satisfactorily explained
   D. show how species behave similarly under the same conditions

10. The migration of lemmings into the sea is an example of

    F. survival of the fittest
    G. population control
    H. self-preservation
    J. natural selection

11. The migration of the nomadic Lapps of Norway is most similar to the migration of

    A. European eels
    B. locusts
    C. Norwegian lemmings
    D. caribou

12. The swallows return each year to the Mission of San Juan Capistrano on St. Joseph's Day because

I. they are religious
II. they are natural hams and know that there are throngs of tourists waiting for them
III. this is the northern terminus of their migration
IV. of a combination of factors

F. I and III
G. II, III, and IV
H. III and IV
J. I, II, III, and IV

A colored transparent object, such as a piece of red glass, transmits red light and absorbs all or most of the other colors that shine on it. But what about opaque (nontransparent) objects? Why is one piece of cloth red, for example, while another is blue? The answer is that we see only the light that is reflected from such an object. White light, which contains all colors, shines on our piece of cloth. The dye in the cloth is of such a nature that it pretty well absorbs all colors except red. The red is then reflected, and that is what we see. If some other color or combination of colors is reflected, then we may get any hue or tint. Incidentally, this gives us a hint as to why many fabrics seem to have one color under artificial light and another color in daylight. The artificial light is of a different composition from daylight, and therefore the amount of each color reflected is different.

Light from an incandescent lamp, for example, contains proportionately more red and yellow than does sunlight, and hence emphasizes the red and yellow hues, weakening the blues and violets by contrast. Strangely enough, though, yellow may appear quite white under an incandescent lamp. This comes about because our eyes, being accustomed to the yellowish light from the lamp, no longer distinguish the lamplight from the real white of sunlight. Therefore, a piece of yellow cloth or paper, reflecting all the colors contained in the lamplight, appears to be white.

13. If an object were manufactured so that all light rays that hit it were reflected away from it, the color of the object would be

    A. white
    B. black
    C. iridescent
    D. transparent

14. If an object absorbed all the light that strikes it, the color of the object would be

    F. white
    G. black
    H. iridescent
    J. transparent

15. If an object were made in such a way that the light striking it was neither reflected nor absorbed, the object would be

    A. white
    B. black
    C. translucent
    D. transparent

16. If the light from a blue mercury lamp which contains no red light waves were to illuminate a pure red tie, the tie would appear to be

    F. white
    G. black
    G. red
    J. transparent

17. The author implies that for an object to be visible

    A. all of the received light must be reflected
    B. some of the received light must be reflected
    C. some of the received light must be absorbed
    D. some of the received light must pass through

18. The phenomenon of seeing an object in its usual color even though the color is distorted by artificial light is called

    F. transformation
    G. compensation
    H. transmutation
    J. assimilation

19. Artificial light
    I. is different from sunlight

    II. contains more red and yellow than sunlight
    III. appears more like sunlight with a green shade
    IV. makes glass transparent

    A. I only
    B. I and II
    C. I, II, and III
    D. I, II, III, and IV

Directions: Questions 20–33 are not based on a reading passage. Choose the *best* answer to each question on the basis of your scientific knowledge.

20. A crystal of anhydrous KNO_3 is made up of

    F. atoms of potassium, nitrogen, and three atoms of oxygen alternately spaced in the crystal
    G. molecules of KNO_3
    H. a geometrical pattern of potassium ions and nitrate ions in the crystal
    J. potassium nitrate molecules alternately spaced with water molecules

21. The loss of a neutron from the nucleus of an atom

    A. changes the chemical nature of the atom
    B. changes a physical property of the atom
    C. causes the subsequent loss of an electron
    D. reduces the atomic number of the atom

22. The number of atoms in $(NH_4)_2CrO_4$ is

    F. 10
    G. 15
    H. 3
    J. 4

23. A block of mass m at the end of a string is whirled around in a vertical circle of radius R. Find the critical speed of the block at the top of its swing below which the string would become slack as the block reaches the top of its swing.

    A. $(Rg)^{1/2}$
    B. Rg
    C. $(Rg)^2$
    D. $\dfrac{R}{g}$

24. A cell part *not* containing any DNA is the

    F. nucleolus
    G. cell vacuole
    H. spindle
    J. mitochondrion

25. Two animals belong to the same species if they

    A. can live together in a similar environment
    B. can mate and produce fertile descendants
    C. show a very close resemblance
    D. come from a common ancestor

26. Which of the following is *not* a colloidal dispersion?

    F. mineral oil
    G. protoplasm
    H. paint
    J. muddy water

27. Seawater can be made suitable for drinking by

    A. coagulation
    B. chlorination
    C. distillation
    D. filtration

28. If 25 ml of an acid are needed to neutralize exactly 50 ml of a 0.2N solution of a base, the normality of the acid is

    F. 0.2

G. 0.4
H. 2.0
J. 4.0

29. Which of the following does *not* belong with the others?

   A. bat
   B. whale
   C. horse
   D. alligator

30. A student in the laboratory tossed two pennies from a container 100 times and recorded these results: both heads, 25; one head and one tail, 47; both tails, 28. Which cross between plants would result in approximately the same ratio?

   F. Aa × AA
   G. Aa × Aa
   H. AA × aa
   J. Aa × aa

31. A girl examining her finger under a microscope could detect no epidermal cells becase

   A. these cells are located under the skin
   B. the nail blocked her view
   C. each single cell is larger than the area of the microscope field
   D. a finger is about one-half inch thick

32. Of the following, the physical property *least* frequently used in chemistry instruction is

   F. taste
   G. odor
   H. solubility
   J. density

33. Sodium is placed on water. The gas given off

   A. supports combustion
   B. turns moist litmus red
   C. burns
   D. has an irritating odor

Sixty high school sophomores were recruited to assist in a learning experiment. Each subject was interviewed and was able to satisfy the experimenters that he or she had no previous experience in the learning of nonsense syllables. The nonsense syllables were to be learned in pairs as MYP—BUB.

The subjects were divided into two types of learning groups. Groups I, II, and III were each handed a long sheet which contained all the pairs of syllables to be learned. In three separate rooms, under close supervision, the students were instructed to silently learn all the pairs. The proctor enforced the silence rule.

The subjects in Group I studied the list for a full hour. The subjects in Group II studied the list for a half hour, then engaged in conversation for a half hour. The subjects in Group III studied the list for ten minutes, then took ten minutes off, studied the list for ten more minutes, alternating study and rest periods of ten minutes for the hour.

Subjects in Groups IV, V, and VI learned the syllables in a very different manner. In three rooms (because of the time variations) they sat before a screen. The first member of a nonsense pair was flashed upon the screen, and all subjects read it aloud. Then the second syllable appeared on the screen with the first, and the subjects read both aloud, in unison.

Subjects in Group IV spent a full hour in this fashion. Subjects in Group V learned the pairs for one-half hour and were free to chat for the other half hour. Subjects in Group VI alternated ten minutes of learning with ten minutes of relaxation. There was a ten-minute break after the hour in which coffee was served to all subjects.

For the test of learning, all subjects sat in the same room before the screen. The first member of each pair of nonsense syllables was flashed upon the screen, and the subjects were required to write on a piece of paper the second member of each pair.

The results were as follows: Subjects in Groups IV, V, and VI all learned better than any subject in Groups I, II and III. The superiority of Groups IV, V, and VI collectively was highly significant. Within each type of learning group, the group that alternated ten minute periods performed best, while the group which learned for one-half hour and talked for one-half hour turned in the poorest results.

In summary, in order of proficiency of learning the groups may be ranked: VI, IV, V, III, I, II.

34. The effects of forgetting were demonstrated by Groups

    F. II and III
    G. V and VI
    H. II and V
    J. III and VI

35. The procedure followed with Groups IV, V, and VI is called

    A. active learning
    B. visual learning
    C. learning through audio-visual technique
    D. passive learning

36. The ten-minute break between learning and testing was offered to all subjects because

    F. the groups learning for a full hour needed a break
    G. the investigators were interested in the effects of coffee upon the learning process
    H. all experiments have a ten-minute break
    J. the coffee was ready

37. The finding that Groups III and VI learned better than Groups I and IV, even though Groups I and IV had a full hour of study as opposed to the total of one-half hour for Groups III and VI shows that

    A. too much practice is harmful
    B. people need practice in "not forgetting"
    C. ten minutes is the maximum length of time in which people can concentrate
    D. distributed practice is more effective than massed practice

38. The most important control in this experiment was

    F. the use of nonsense syllables
    G. giving everyone the same amount of time from the first exposure to the syllables until the test
    H. correlating the learning times of Groups IV, V, and VI with the learning times of Groups I, II, and III
    J. the serving of coffee

39. An important uncontrolled factor was

    A. the possibility that some subjects might prefer tea
    B. how loudly the subjects in Groups IV, V, and VI pronounced the syllables
    C. the possibility of subvocalization by subjects in Groups I, II, and III
    D. the intelligence of the subjects

40. The purpose of this experiment was to
    I. determine the best way to teach nonsense syllables
    II. find out which nonsense syllables are easiest to learn
    III. discover the effects of massed versus distributed learning
    IV. find out what kind of learning procedure is best

    F. I and II
    G. III and IV
    H. I, III, and IV
    J. II, III, and IV

41. If schools were to utilize the information presented by the superior learning of Groups IV, V, and VI, they would

    A. show more movies
    B. offer regular coffee breaks
    C. have teachers read aloud to the students
    D. schedule more periods per student in the science labs

42. The results of this experiment imply that passive rote memorization of whole units is

    F. good
    G. bad
    H. inefficient
    J. totally useless

43. Occasional breaks from study

    A. are good because they allow time to assimilate and integrate that which was learned
    B. are bad because they give time to forget
    C. are good because they give time to drink coffee, which is an aid to studying
    D. are bad because they just waste valuable time

44. The student who takes these results seriously will

F. go to the movies the night before an exam

G. cram for the last 24 hours before an exam

H. study and review periodically throughout the term

J. read all materials aloud

Throughout the history of our planet, natural phenomena have played an important role in determining the contours of the earth, the distribution of the waters, and the nature of life supported in the various regions.

Within known history, natural catastrophes have affected the lives of millions of people. Some of these catastrophes have caused widespread death and destruction. Others have forced us to alter our ways to conform to the demands of nature.

Despite all of our advanced technologies, we have not devised any method for reversal of natural phenomena. We cannot prevent or halt an earthquake or a volcanic eruption. We cannot cause rain to fall in a period of severe drought, nor cause the rain to stop when floods rampage over the land.

Since, much as we may try, we seem unable to alter natural phenomena, we have diverted our energies into learning to cope with them. These efforts have met with varying degrees of success. Irrigation systems have given relief in areas of consistent drought, but are of no use where sudden, unexpected drought strikes for a prolonged number of years. Hurricanes are predicted and tracked so that people in their paths may scurry to safety, but the hurricane may shift its path erratically and strike unprepared areas. Seismographic reports of suboceanic earth shifts may help to predict tsunamis, but the warning may come too late.

The recent eruption of Mount St. Helens in the state of Washington has led to renewed research into the nature of volcanos, the causes of their eruptions after hundreds of years of dormancy, and the possibilities of preventing such eruptions. Consideration has been given to procedures for rupturing the plugs in the throats of volcanos, thus relieving pressure before it builds to a violent explosion. Innovative scientists are also giving thought to the feasibility of opening volcanic arteries in the sides of such mountains, if those arteries can be identified, and allowing the lava to flow harmlessly down a predetermined path.

A more frightening outgrowth of our advanced technology is our ability to induce natural phenomena, not to simulate these events, but to actually create them. The building of dams with the subsequent creation of huge artificial lakes has caused earthquakes in Colorado, Africa, and India. These earthquakes, in areas which had never before experienced such phenomena, were probably caused by the weight of water in areas unaccustomed to such weight. Man-made earthquakes are not necessarily insignificant tremors. The 1967 earthquake near the Koyna Dam in India killed 177 people.

Earthquakes have also been triggered by nuclear explosions, and by the drilling of very deep (two or more miles) wells and then pumping into them large quantities of water polluted with toxic wastes. The fact that pumping water deep into the earth can cause earthquakes has led scientists to explore the possibility of using carefully placed injections of water for earthquake control.

With our new technological capabilities, we have even created a geyser. In 1955, an operation in Oregon working for geothermal power bored through a layer of sand and brought up a jet of hot water. This geyser, named Crump Well, has continued to this date to spout a jet of water one hundred feet into the air precisely once every nine hours.

45. The natural phenomena which have determined the contours of the earth have included

I. movement of ice caps
II. traveling of continents
III. death of the dinosaurs
IV. erosion

A. I only
B. I and II
C. I, II, and IV
D. I, II, III, and IV

46. A tsunami is a (an)

   F. tidal wave
   G. earthquake
   H. typhoon
   J. tornado

47. A seismograph measures

   A. wind velocity
   B. hurricane intensity
   C. earth tremors
   D. earth temperature

48. A major difference between a volcano and a geyser is that

   F. the steam produced by a volcano is hotter
   G. eruption of geysers is predictable and rhythmic
   H. geysers are in uninhabited areas
   J. volcanos are releases of built-up pressure

49. The eruption of a geyser consists of

   A. distilled water
   B. cool mineral water and spray
   C. hot water and steam
   D. water and pebbles

50. Earthquakes are caused by
   I. artificial water pressure
   II. water pollution
   III. natural forces not completely understood
   IV. volcanic eruptions

   F. I and III
   G. II and IV
   H. I, II, and III
   J. II, III, and IV

51. The tone of this article is

   A. ebullient and optimistic
   B. pessimistic
   C. cautionary but optimistic
   D. neutral

52. A tidal wave is

   F. caused by action of the moon
   G. very swift-moving
   H. affected by the action of sun spots
   J. usually caused by underwater nuclear explosions

END OF EXAM

If you complete this test before the time is up, check back over the
questions on this test only. Do not return to any previous tests.

ANSWER KEY

Test 1.   English Usage

1. (A)	16. (F)	31. (B)	46. (F)	61. (D)
2. (F)	17. (C)	32. (J)	47. (A)	62. (G)
3. (D)	18. (F)	33. (D)	48. (F)	63. (C)
4. (H)	19. (D)	34. (J)	49. (D)	64. (G)
5. (B)	20. (G)	35. (C)	50. (J)	65. (D)
6. (J)	21. (C)	36. (F)	51. (B)	66. (J)
7. (D)	22. (J)	37. (B)	52. (G)	67. (A)
8. (G)	23. (D)	38. (J)	53. (A)	68. (J)
9. (C)	24. (J)	39. (B)	54. (F)	69. (C)
10. (H)	25. (B)	40. (J)	55. (A)	70. (F)
11. (B)	26. (F)	41. (C)	56. (J)	71. (B)
12. (J)	27. (C)	42. (J)	57. (A)	72. (J)
13. (D)	28. (J)	43. (D)	58. (J)	73. (B)
14. (G)	29. (B)	44. (G)	59. (A)	74. (H)
15. (A)	30. (H)	45. (A)	60. (H)	75. (A)

Test 2.   Mathematics Usage

1. (B)	9. (E)	17. (D)	25. (D)	33. (B)
2. (J)	10. (H)	18. (F)	26. (K)	34. (G)
3. (A)	11. (D)	19. (B)	27. (B)	35. (D)
4. (J)	12. (K)	20. (J)	28. (J)	36. (J)
5. (E)	13. (E)	21. (A)	29. (A)	37. (A)
6. (H)	14. (K)	22. (H)	30. (F)	38. (G)
7. (D)	15. (D)	23. (B)	31. (E)	39. (C)
8. (H)	16. (K)	24. (J)	32. (H)	40. (F)

Test 3.   Social Studies Reading

1. (A)	14. (F)	27. (D)	40. (H)
2. (G)	15. (C)	28. (F)	41. (C)
3. (D)	16. (J)	29. (A)	42. (G)
4. (G)	17. (D)	30. (F)	43. (D)
5. (C)	18. (H)	31. (D)	44. (H)
6. (F)	19. (A)	32. (F)	45. (D)
7. (D)	20. (F)	33. (B)	46. (F)
8. (H)	21. (D)	34. (H)	47. (A)
9. (D)	22. (J)	35. (C)	48. (G)
10. (G)	23. (B)	36. (J)	49. (D)
11. (B)	24. (H)	37. (D)	50. (J)
12. (H)	25. (C)	38. (G)	51. (B)
13. (B)	26. (J)	39. (D)	52. (J)

Test 4.   Natural Science Reading

1.	(C)	14.	(G)	27.	(C)	40.	(G)
2.	(G)	15.	(C)	28.	(G)	41.	(D)
3.	(B)	16.	(G)	29.	(D)	42.	(H)
4.	(F)	17.	(A)	30.	(G)	43.	(A)
5.	(C)	18.	(G)	31.	(D)	44.	(H)
6.	(F)	19.	(A)	32.	(F)	45.	(C)
7.	(B)	20.	(H)	33.	(C)	46.	(F)
8.	(H)	21.	(B)	34.	(H)	47.	(C)
9.	(C)	22.	(G)	35.	(A)	48.	(G)
10.	(G)	23.	(A)	36.	(F)	49.	(C)
11.	(D)	24.	(G)	37.	(D)	50.	(F)
12.	(H)	25.	(B)	38.	(F)	51.	(C)
13.	(A)	26.	(F)	39.	(C)	52.	(G)

EXPLANATORY ANSWERS

Test 1. English Usage

1. **(A)** The idiom is correctly written. *Another* is always one word.

2. **(F)** *Everyone* is singular, therefore the pronoun must be singular. Furthermore, none of the incorrect choices is a legitimate word.

3. **(D)** Avoid use of the word *you* when not addressing a specific person or group of people.

4. **(H)** As in question 3, avoid the use of *you*.

5. **(B)** A question must end with a question mark.

6. **(J)** Again, see question 3.

7. **(D)** The sentence is incorrect as written because *careful* is an adjective and what is needed is an adverb to modify the verb *study*. Choices (B) and (C) are correct but awkward. Since studying implies care, no modifying adverb is required.

8. **(G)** The possessive form of *it* is *its*. *It's* is the contraction for *it is*. *The English language* is singular.

9. **(C)** The author is introducing a new idea, so a new paragraph is required. There is no quoted material.

10. **(H)** *English* is the name of the language, so it must be capitalized. There is no reason to capitalize the adjective *good*. Choice (J) is verbose.

11. **(B)** *This contention* is singular, so the singular verb *is* must be used. The correct contraction for *is not* is *isn't*.

12. **(J)** *It* is an expletive (a pronoun subject with no antecedent). An expletive is always weak, especially when it occurs in the middle of a sentence. Unless a sentence is compound, try to maintain the same subject throughout the sentence, as in (J).

13. **(D)** Because the passage continues from choice

(J) of question 12, the subject *he* has already been stated. *Correct* is an adjective and thus cannot modify the verb *speak*.

14. **(G)** *Who* is the subject of the verb *to speak*. *Which* cannot apply to people.

15. **(A)** The subject, *words and phrases,* is plural, requiring use of the plural verb *say*. *Who* cannot refer to things. *What* is not a relative pronoun.

16. **(F)** *Than* is a pronoun expressing comparison. *Then* is an adverb expressing progression in time.

17. **(C)** *Hard-to-understand* is a made-up adjective, and its parts must be connected by hyphens.

18. **(F)** The author is speaking of his present state; he is not recounting a past event. The present perfect tense is suited for the situation.

19. **(D)** One does not publish one's own telephone number. *Listing* is a gerund and therefore acts as a noun and should be modified by the adjective *your*.

20. **(G)** Normally an introductory prepositional phrase need not be separated by a comma unless it contains five or more words. In this sentence, however, *in other words* has a somewhat parenthetical sense and should be set off by a comma.

21. **(C)** *Claim* is a clearer verb than the general *say*. Choices (A) and (B) are extremely verbose.

22. **(J)** This choice is most succinct.

23. **(D)** The additional expense is a result of the special recordkeeping and handling of requests, not vice-versa as implied in (A) and (B).

24. **(J)** The phrase is referring to *an unpublished number* (see question 22). (F) is incorrect because it does not maintain agreement in number. The pronoun in (H) is an unwise choice, for the antecedent is too distant.

25. **(B)** All other choices are verbose.

26. **(F)** The term *percent* (also *per cent*) is derived from the Latin term *per centum*. Use of the Latin term is technically correct but is quite stilted in ordinary use. The percent sign is used only in technical writing.

27. **(C)** Since calls are discrete events that can be counted, *fewer* is the correct adjective.

28. **(J)** The phrase is unnecessary.

29. **(B)** When two independent clauses are separated by a coordinating conjunction, the conjunction should be preceded by a comma. Setting off *therefore* with commas is optional.

30. **(H)** See explanation for question 29.

31. **(B)** A semicolon NEVER precedes a coordinating conjunction. A comma may not be followed by a capital letter (unless the word is a proper noun). (A) is incorrect because a comma would be required before the coordinating conjunction. The strong statement may legitimately be punctuated with an exclamation point. The subsequent new sentence begins with a capital letter.

32. **(J)** A written sentence should not end with a preposition.

33. **(D)** Because the word *charge* is so far away, the antecedent of the pronoun is unclear; therefore repeat the noun. Unless the desired antecedent is the last noun stated, the best policy is usually to repeat the noun.

34. **(J)** This answer requires looking ahead. The company "gets away with murder" in *spite* of the anti-trust law, not because of it; therefore 35 (C) is correct. In conjunction with 35 (C), 34 (J) is the only logical answer.

35. **(C)** See question 34.

36. **(F)** In question 35 we eliminated a time frame; therefore, use a simple present tense as in question 34.

37. **(B)** *Lest* is the correct word in this construction.

38. **(J)** *We consumers* is the subject of the verb *are*. *Us* can only be an object. *We, the consumer*, lacks agreement in number.

39. **(B)** An introductory subordinate clause is followed by a comma.

40. **(J)** The sentence must make sense.

41. **(C)** *Better Business Bureau* is a singular noun and therefore the correct pronoun is *it*. Expletive construction as in (B) should be avoided whenever possible.

42. **(J)** (F) and (G) are unclear. *Against* is the wrong preposition.

43. **(D)** All other choices have missing or misplaced apostrophes.

44. **(G)** All other choices are verbose and awkward.

45. **(A)** (B) has a different meaning. (C) and (D) are grammatically incorrect.

46. **(F)** One *brings* something *here;* one *takes* it *there*. *Bring* requires an indirect object or a word acting in that capacity.

47. **(A)** (C) and (D) are not words. (B) implies that *things* acquire their values from science.

48. **(F)** *U.S.A.* is a correct abbreviation. *US* would require periods. If the name of the country is spelled out, all the major words must begin with capital letters.

49. **(D)** *Our* is the possessive adjective form of *we*.

50. **(J)** We have only one country and it is singular.

51. **(B)** The two independent clauses must be separated by a semicolon. *They're* is the contraction for *they are*.

52. **(G)** There is no reason for a possessive form. Citizenship is irrelevant in the context of the sentence.

53. **(A)** All other choices would leave the main clause of the sentence without a verb.

54. **(F)** There is no reason for a hyphen or for a capital *S*. The sea has no feelings, so cannot be bored.

55. **(A)** There is no reason for a hyphen nor for a capital *V*. The apostrophe is unnecessary as *Mississippi valley* is an acceptable term.

56. **(J)** *Wild* is an adjective modifying *birds.* The word *wildbird* does not exist.

57. **(A)** If the birds were *never seen,* the author would not know about them. The phrase *never before captured* implies that they recently were.

58. **(J)** The past tense of the verb *to bring* is *brought.*

59. **(A)** The *Yankees* as a team were defeated, not any particular Yankee. The statement is not an exclamation.

60. **(H)** The *Rangers* create double plays as a team. *Double play* is two words. A comma is needed before a coordinating conjunction separating complete clauses.

61. **(D)** (D) is more succinct than (A). (B) and (C) change the meaning.

62. **(G)** All other choices are incorrect because *style* does not *make plays.*

63. **(C)** No punctuation is needed, but an adverb is.

64. **(G)** The idiom is *as if.*

65. **(D)** A statement contrary to fact (he was not using a broom) requires the subjunctive.

66. **(J)** *Who* and *whom* refer only to people. *What* is not a relative pronoun.

67. **(A)** *When* is a better word than *if* because it puts the sentence into a time frame. The word *and* provides necessary transition.

68. **(J)** One *figures upon* an abacus or calculator. *Estimate* is the wrong word; if *Jones* strikes out, you are *sure of* the pitching strength.

69. **(C)** The past tense of the verb *to find* is *found.* As the author is recounting a past incident, the past tense, not the present perfect, is correct.

70. **(F)** The *team* is a collective noun taking the singular pronoun *it.* The possessive form of *it* is *its.* *It's* is the contraction for *it is.*

71. **(B)** The *Rangers* are referred to as a group of individuals, so the correct pronoun is *their. There* refers to place.

72. **(J)** The verb must be parallel. Since New York *had* a team last year, it *has* a team this year.

73. **(B)** Eastern or Western Division refers to the American League and should therefore be placed directly after it.

74. **(H)** The *team* is singular, thus *has* is correct. (F) constitutes use of a double negative. (J) is verbose.

75. **(A)** No punctuation is needed. *Its* is the possessive form of *it. It's* is the contraction for *it is.*

Test 2. Mathematics Usage

1. **(B)** $40\% = \dfrac{2}{5}$

$$\dfrac{2}{5} \times \dfrac{10}{7} = \dfrac{4}{7}$$

2. **(J)** 27 and 51 are each divisible by 3. 17 and 59 are prime numbers.

3. **(A)** Angle DOC = 6 + x
Angle AOC = (6 + x) + x = 180 − 20
6 + 2x = 160
2x = 154
x = 77

4. **(J)** Let C = the capacity in gallons.
Then $\frac{1}{3}C + 3 = \frac{1}{2}C$
Multiplying through by 6, we obtain
2C + 18 = 3C
or C = 18

5. **(E)** $\dfrac{91 + 88 + 86 + 78 + x}{5} = 85$

343 + x = 425
x = 82

6. **(H)** $12 \times .39 = 4.68$ inches; that is, between $4\frac{1}{2}$ and 5.

7. **(D)**

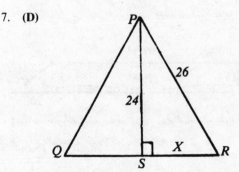

In the figure, PS⊥QR. Then, in right triangle PSR,

$$x^2 + 24^2 = 26^2$$
$$x^2 = 26^2 - 24^2$$
$$= (26 + 24)(26 - 24)$$
$$x^2 = 50 \cdot 2 = 100$$
$$x = 10$$

Thus, QR = 20

8. **(H)** All terms involving x are 0. Hence, the equation reduces to $0 - 7y + 15 = 0$ or $7y = 15$.

$$y = 2\frac{1}{7}$$

9. **(E)** Let s = number of shirts and t = number of string ties, where s and t are integers.
Then $7s + 3t = 81$
$$7s = 81 - 3t$$
$$s = \frac{81 - 3t}{7}$$

Since s is an integer, t must have an integral value such that $81 - 3t$ is divisible by 7. Trial shows that t = 6 is the smallest such number,

making $s = \frac{81 - 18}{7} = \frac{63}{7} = 9$
$$s : t = 9 : 6$$
$$= 3 : 2$$

10. **(H)** rate $= \dfrac{\text{distance}}{\text{time}} = \dfrac{\frac{2}{5} \text{ mile}}{\frac{5}{60} \text{ hour}} = \dfrac{\frac{2}{5}}{\frac{1}{12}}$

rate $= \dfrac{2}{5} \cdot \dfrac{12}{1} = \dfrac{24}{5} = 4\frac{4}{5}$ miles per hour

11. **(D)** Draw the altitudes indicated. A rectangle and two right triangles are produced. From the figure, the base of each triangle is 20 feet. By the Pythagorean theorem, the altitude is 15 feet. Hence, the area

$K = \frac{1}{2} \cdot 15 (100 + 140)$

$= \frac{1}{2} \cdot 15 \cdot 240$

$= 15 \cdot 120$

$= 1800$ square feet

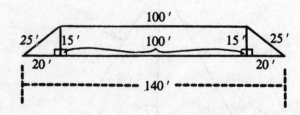

12. **(K)** If $1 + \dfrac{1}{t} = \dfrac{t + 1}{1}$, then the right hand fraction can also be reduced to $1 + \dfrac{1}{t}$, and we have an identity which is true for all values of t except 0.

13. **(E)** All points 6 inches from A are on a circle of radius 6 with the center at A. All points 1 inch from b are on 2 straight lines parallel to b and 1 inch from it on each side. These two parallel lines intersect the circle in 4 points.

14. **(K)** Let R = 5P and S = 5Q where P and Q are integers. Then, (F), $R - S = 5P - 5Q = 5(P - Q)$ is divisible by 5. (G), $RS = 5P \times 5Q = 25PG$ is divisible by 25. (H), $R + S = 5P + 5Q = 5(P + Q)$ is divisible by 5. (J), $R^2 + S^2 = 25P^2 + 25Q^2 = 25(P^2 + Q^2)$ is divisible by 5. (K), $R + S = 5P + 5Q = 5(P + Q)$, which is not necessarily divisible by 10.

15. **(D)** $\frac{1}{2} \cdot 7 \cdot h = \pi \cdot 7^2$. Dividing both sides by 7, we get $\frac{1}{2}h = 7\pi$ or $h = 14\pi$.

16. **(K)**

$$\frac{9}{13} = 13\overline{)9.00} \begin{array}{r} .69 \\ \underline{78} \\ 120 \\ \underline{117} \end{array}$$

$$\frac{13}{9} = 9\overline{)13.00} \begin{array}{r} 1.44 \\ \underline{9} \\ 40 \\ \underline{36} \\ 40 \\ \underline{36} \end{array}$$

70% = .7

$$\frac{1}{.70} = \frac{1}{\frac{7}{10}} = \frac{10}{7}\overline{)10.00} \begin{array}{r} 1.42 \\ \underline{7} \\ 30 \\ \underline{28} \\ 20 \end{array}$$

Correct order is $\dfrac{9}{13}$, 70%, $\dfrac{1}{.70}$, $\dfrac{13}{9}$ or I, III, IV, II.

17. **(D)**

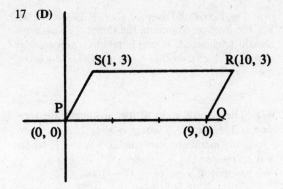

21. **(A)** Let x = the cost.

Then $x + \frac{1}{4}x = 80$

$4x + x = 320$

$5x = 320$

$= \$64 \text{ (cost)}$

$\dfrac{\text{Cost}}{\text{S.P.}} = \dfrac{64}{80}$

$= \dfrac{4}{5}$

Since PQ and RS are parallel and equal, the figure is a parallelogram of base = 9 and height = 3. Hence, area = 9 · 3 = 27.

18. **(F)**

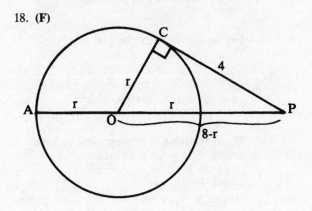

22. **(H)**

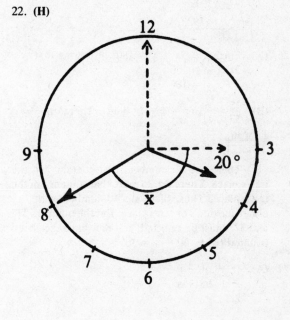

From the figure, in right triangle PCO,

$PO^2 = r^2 + 4^2$

$(8 - r)^2 = r^2 + 16$

$64 - 16r + r^2 = r^2 + 16$

$48 = 16r$

$r = 3$

$6 = \text{diameter}$

At 3:00, the large hand is at 12 and the small hand is at 3. During the next 40 minutes, the large hand moves to 8 and the small hand moves $\frac{40}{60} = \frac{2}{3}$ of the distance between 3 and 4; $\frac{2}{3} \times 30° = 20°$. Since there are 30° between two numbers of a clock $\measuredangle x = 5(30°) - 20° = 150° - 20° = 130°$.

19. **(B)** Area of wall = $4 \cdot \dfrac{60}{3} = 4 \cdot 20 = 80$ sq. yd.

Cost = 80 × \$10.50 = \$840.00

20. **(J)** Distance of (4,4) from origin =
$\sqrt{16 + 16} = \sqrt{32} < 7$

Distance of (5,5) from origin =
$\sqrt{25 + 25} = \sqrt{50} > 7$

Distance of (4,5) from origin =
$\sqrt{16 + 25} = \sqrt{41} < 7$

Distance of (4,6) from origin =
$\sqrt{16 + 36} = \sqrt{52} > 7$

Hence, only II and IV are outside circle.

23. **(B)** Area of sector $= \dfrac{120}{360} \cdot \pi \cdot 15^2$

$= \dfrac{1}{3} \cdot \pi \cdot 15 \cdot 15$

$= 75\pi$

24. **(J)** $\dfrac{17}{10}y = 0.51$

Multiplying both sides by 10, we get

$17y = 5.1$

$y = .3$

25. **(D)** $40\% = \frac{2}{5} \times 50 = 20$ girls attended

$50\% = \frac{1}{2} \times 70 = 35$ boys attended

Total attended = 55

$\frac{55}{50 + 70} = \frac{55}{120} =$

$\frac{11}{24}$ .458 = 45.8%
24)11.000
     96
    ‾‾‾‾‾
    140
    120
    ‾‾‾‾‾
     200
     192

26. **(K)** Since $x + 2x + y = 180°$, it follows that
$$3x + y = 180$$
$$y = 180 - 3x$$

27. **(B)** $\frac{18}{33} = \frac{6}{11}$. $6^2 = 36$; $11^2 = 121$. Therefore $\frac{\sqrt{6^2}}{\sqrt{11^2}}$

$= \frac{\sqrt{36}}{\sqrt{121}}$.

28. **(J)** There are 20 numbers that contain 7 in the one's place. There are 20 more that contain 7 in the ten's place. Thus, there are 40 numbers with 7 in either the one's or ten's place. But the numbers 277 and 377 must be rejected, and they have each been counted twice. $40 - 4 = 36$.

29. **(A)** $(r + s)^2 - r^2 - s^2 =$
$r^2 + 2rs + s^2 - r^2 - s^2 =$
$2rs$

30. **(F)** As Q moves from R to S, PQ gets smaller. Its largest possible value would be 9. Hence $9 \geq PQ \geq 6$.

31. **(E)** selling price per article $= \frac{K}{8}$

cost per article $= \frac{K}{12}$

profit per article $= \frac{K}{8} - \frac{K}{12} = \frac{3K - 2K}{24} = \frac{K}{24}$

32. **(H)** Analyze this by means of the diagram below:

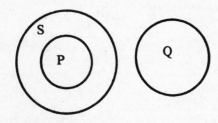

From the figure, we readily see that no P are Q.

33. **(B)** The sum of the four numbers is $45 \times 4 = 180$. For the average to remain the same, the sum must remain unchanged. If one number is increased by 6, then each of the other three must be reduced by 2.

34. **(G)** The general term of this arithmetic progression is $3 + 9(n - 1)$ where $n = 1, 2, 3, \ldots$ etc. Thus, any member must equal $3 + 9(n - 1)$ where n is an integer.
We see that, if $9 + 3(n - 1) = 10002$
then $3(n - 1) = 9993$
and $n - 1 = 3331$
or $n = 3332$
Thus, 10,002 will be a member of the series.

35. **(D)** The papers drawn will be numbered 4, 11, 18, 25, 32, 39. Number 39 will be the last.

36. **(J)** Let the angles be 2x, 3x, and 5x.
Then $2x + 3x + 5x = 180°$
$$10x = 180°$$
$$x = 18$$
$5x = 90°$ and the triangle is right.

37. **(A)** The dimensions of the open box become:
length $= 24 - 10 = 14$ inches
width $= 18 - 10 = 8$ inches
height $= 5$ inches
Hence, $V = 14 \cdot 8 \cdot 5 = 560$ cubic inches.

38. **(G)** $VT = 32$ feet, so $ST = \frac{1}{2}VT = 16$ feet.
Therefore, in right triangle QST, the legs are 12 and 16. Right triangles can be expressed in a 3-4-5 ratio. $12 = 4 \cdot 3$, $16 = 4 \cdot 4$, and therefore hypotenuse QT equals $4 \cdot 5$, 20. Adding 1 foot for the overhang yields 21 feet.

39. **(C)** Form the proportion $\frac{\frac{3}{4}}{9} = \frac{\frac{7}{8}}{x}$, where x is the side in miles.

Then $\frac{3}{4}x = \frac{7}{8} \cdot 9$. Multiply both sides by 8.
$6x = 7 \cdot 9 = 63$
$x = 10\frac{1}{2}$ miles

Area $= x^2 = \frac{21}{2} \cdot \frac{21}{2} = \frac{441}{4} = 110\frac{1}{2}$ square miles

40. **(F)** Give $V = fL$, divide both sides by f. $L = \frac{V}{f}$

Test 3.   Social Studies Reading

1. **(A)**   The author of this article is stating both sides of a controversial matter in an objective manner.

2. **(G)**   While English teachers certainly notice the effects of television on the reading habits and the thoughts of their students, the specific phenomenon of the soaps is not of scientific interest to them. Likewise, historians might take notice of the phenomenon, but not because of scientific interest. Sociologists would be interested in the nature of a society which produces this type of activity. Social psychologists would probe the needs served by collective watching of soap operas.

3. **(D)**   Again, since many reasons are given for watching soap operas, the one certain factor is that teenage fascination with the soaps is a new fad.

4. **(G)**   Rationalization is providing plausible, reasonable, but untrue reasons for one's behavior. It is unlikely that people watch soap operas so that they may avoid gossiping about each other.

5. **(C)**   This question takes liberties with the definition of *instinct.* The instinct served by the watching of soap operas is *aggregation,* the instinct to be part of the group.

6. **(F)**   The objections to *habitual* watching of soap operas center about the dulling effect on the mind and the wasted time which might be better spent on extracurricular activities or individual mind-stretching occupations.

7. **(D)**   The first soap operas were on the radio, sponsored by laundry products, and the name has come to be applied to all serialized melodramas.

8. **(H)**   The English teacher feels that relaxation and recreation are necessary, but there are more constructive outlets available than the mindless watching of soaps.

9. **(D)**   Actual election of the President is by the electors according to provision of the Constitution.

10. **(G)**   The Constitution provides that the total number of electors to which a state is entitled is the combined number of Representatives and Senators.

11. **(B)**   The Constitution provides that the ballots of the electors be opened by the President of the Senate. The Vice President of the United States is the President of the Senate.

12. **(H)**   The Constitution provides that ". . . no Senator or Representative, or Person holding an Office of Trust or Profit under the United States, shall be appointed an Elector." A state's governor is an official of that state only.

13. **(B)**   It is possible for the popular vote to be so distributed that a candidate might win the majority of the electoral votes while winning only 45 percent of the popular vote. This might happen if the candidate were to earn the electoral votes of some of the most populous states by very slim margins while losing many other states very decisively.

14. **(F)**   The Constitution requires that the ballots be sent to "the Seat of the Government of the United States." The seat of government is Washington, D.C.

15. **(C)**   There are people who consider the electoral system undemocratic, mainly because of the possibility of a *minority President,* that is, a President who was not chosen by a majority of the people. Electing the President by popular vote would eliminate this criticism.

16. **(J)**   The Constitution sets no limits on the number of candidates for the presidency, nor does it make any mention of political parties.

17. **(D)**   The Constitution provides that an elector must vote for at least one candidate from a state other than his own. If candidates for both President and Vice President were to come from the same state, the electors from that state would be disenfranchised, prohibited from voting for both of them. The Constitution does not actually prohibit one state from monopolizing the White House and, theoretically it might have happened before 1804, at which time President and Vice President were winner and runner-up rather than candidates for two positions. Choice (B) is also correct, but it is not the *best* answer.

18. **(H)**   The problems created by having President and Vice President of opposing parties and often in philosophical disagreement on crucial issues led to the Twelfth Amendment. Under this Amendment, electors vote separately for a President and a Vice

President and are expected to have the good sense to not put political rivals into office together. The Twelfth Amendment restates the requirement that an elector must vote for one candidate from a state other than his own.

19. **(A)** The spelling, capitalization, and punctuation of the Constitution were all correct at the time of writing (in 1787). The apparent anomaly of more than one person's having a majority of the vote is clarified when one remembers that the Constitution provides that each elector cast separate votes for two people. Since the passage of the Twelfth Amendment, which requires that each elector cast one vote for a President-Vice President slate, it is no longer possible for more than one candidate to win a majority of the votes.

20. **(F)** ". . . then the House of Representatives shall immediately chuse by Ballot one of them for President." The implication is that this should be done at the time of the counting of the ballots.

21. **(D)** The electoral college is the semantic term referring to all the electors in their role as electors.

22. **(J)** The Constitution grants discretion to each state legislature to direct that electors be appointed according to rules of its own making.

23. **(B)** The basic quarrel between these two speakers has to do with government control, the need for it or its excessive use with regard to our economy.

24. **(H)** While Speaker Number One believes in free competition, his antipathy toward government interference is so great that he most certainly would be opposed to regulation of industry by the Sherman Anti-Trust Act. In fact, with his attitude that "business will do what is best," he would accept monopolies as being in the best interests of business.

25. **(C)** While Speaker Number One would certainly not be happy with strikes which interfered with business, he would accept them as being part of the natural process and would oppose government efforts to settle them.

26. **(J)** Speaker Number Two is concerned with the economic plight of the aged and the poor. The Sales Tax is a regressive tax in that it falls equally upon the poor and the rich, thus constituting a greater burden to the poor. Speaker Two specifically proposes the Income Tax, which ostensibly falls more heavily upon these more able to pay.

27. **(D)** Speaker Number Two feels that government controls are necessary in a complex economy. Speaker Number One feels that government controls are never the answer.

28. **(F)** *Laissez-faire,* a French term meaning "let the people do as they please," is a doctrine opposing government interference in economic affairs beyond the minimum necessary for maintaining property rights.

29. **(A)** The speakers would not agree as to the means for avoiding swings in the business cycles, but both would agree that ups and downs in the economy are not desirable.

30. **(F)** OSHA (Occupational Safety and Health Administration) is responsible for the health and safety of workers on their jobs. The FHA (Federal Housing Administration) grants low-cost guaranteed mortgages to certain people who might otherwise be unable to purchase houses. Both of these agencies would represent government interference to Speaker Number One. There is no reason to assume that Speaker Number One would oppose the CIA (Central Intelligence Agency), an intelligence gathering agency, or the FDIC (Federal Deposit Insurance Corporation), which provides insurance for bank deposits in national and state banks that are members of the Federal Reserve system.

31. **(D)** Speaker Number Two would consider both OSHA and FHA to be useful, humanitarian organizations. There is no reason to believe that Speaker Number Two would oppose the security efforts of the CIA or the insurance provided by the FDIC.

32. **(F)** The Northwest Ordinance, passed by Congress in 1787, provided for the administration of United States territories in what is now the Midwest, and provided for the eventual creation by Congress of three to five states in this area. The new states were to be admitted to the Union as equals of the original states.

33. **(B)** The 3/5 Compromise provided that five slaves would be considered equal to three white persons in determining the representation of the states in the House of Representatives and also for apportioning taxes. This compromise was a concession to the southern states.

34. **(H)** In 1811–1812, a group of Congressmen representing the West gained control of the House of

Representatives. Their two most important leaders were Henry Clay and John C. Calhoun. Clay and Calhoun advocated a war with England to have the opportunity to annex Canada.

35. **(C)** Russia was not involved in post-World War I peace conferences.

36. **(J)** Depreciation, while not a visible cost to a firm, must be written off during each fiscal period in order to record accurately the expense of capital deterioration. All the others are explicit, visible costs.

37. **(D)** Delinquent gangs arise chiefly out of informal childhood play groups, following roughly the same dynamics that affect the development of nondelinquent gangs. The nature of a gang is determined by its leadership and is influenced by social and economic circumstances. Membership is based upon geographical contiguity rather than on shared abnormalities of the members.

38. **(G)** Texas was annexed by a joint resolution of Congress in 1845, several days before President Tyler left office. The resolution was signed by President Polk in December 1845. The Treaty of Guadalupe Hidalgo ended the Mexican War, February 2, 1848.

39. **(D)** From 1862 to 1865, 170,000 blacks served in the Union Army. Former slaves were not prevented from joining the army nor from entering combat. The 13th Amendment did not affect black troops during the Civil War since it did not come about until the war was over. During the first year of the war, the Union Army rejected black troops; Lincoln feared that the arming of blacks would not be well received. Black soldiers were accepted in the army in 1862 and thereafter were formed into black regiments, generally led by white officers. Blacks could and did, however, attain officer rank during the war.

40. **(H)** Immigrants in urban areas organized burial and insurance societies. Public schools, political parties, and settlement houses were not self-help organizations initiated by immigrants themselves, but were institutions established by society.

41. **(C)** The *Plessy* v. *Ferguson* decision of 1896 upheld a Louisiana statute to enforce racial segregation in railroad cars. The decision supported the "separate but equal" doctrine and encouraged further legislation to enforce segregation of blacks in public facilities. The court contended that the 14th Amendment was intended to enforce equality but not to abolish social distinctions. The case of *Brown* v. *Board of Education* in 1954 effectively reversed the decision in *Plessy* v. *Ferguson,* at least insofar as education is concerned, by declaring that separate is by its nature unequal. *Muller* v. *Oregon* was a case concerning the constitutionality of labor laws which apply solely to women. *Gibbons* v. *Ogden* was a case in interstate commerce regulation.

42. **(G)** The United States and England continued to disagree about many issues even following the Treaty of Paris, but the impressment of American seamen was not one of those issues at that time. England began seizing American ships and impressing seamen into service of the Crown during the Napoleanic Wars, at which time England hoped to suppress American trade with France.

43. **(D)** England and the Netherlands were both Protestant nations, hence religious differences never presented a problem. The two seafaring nations were rivals in all areas concerning fishing, trade, and colonialism.

44. **(H)** The League of Nations was established in 1919 under the terms of the Versailles Treaty. The formula for the League had first been presented by President Wilson in his "Fourteen Points" speech before Congress in 1918. The Treaty and American membership in the League of Nations were defeated by the Senate in 1919 and 1920, much to the chagrin of President Wilson.

45. **(D)** The first sentence states the theme and purpose of the passage. English voting laws were the basis for American voting laws.

46. **(F)** Loss of power by the King led to increased power in the hands of the people, initially the landed gentry. The shift from an agricultural, somewhat feudal, economy to an industrial economy caused further change in the seat of power.

47. **(A)** In England, land ownership was prerequisite to political power. All land not inherited could be obtained only through purchase, thus economic means led to political power.

48. **(G)** With industrialization, the economy ceased being based upon exchange of goods and services and instead became based upon money. It was money that enabled citizens to buy the land and obtain the education necessary for acquiring voting rights as defined in the 1689 bill.

49. **(D)** Prior to the industrialization and the money economy, land ownership was strictly hereditary.

50. **(J)** The 1689 English "Bill of Rights" was passed just as the King began to lose his absolute power. Without an orderly means for distributing this power, anarchy might have prevailed. Further, this Bill was still highly restrictive, granting some share of power to only a privileged few. By signing the Bill, the King hoped to maintain control and keep dilution of royal power to a minimum.

51. **(B)** It seems unlikely that the King willingly gave up his absolute power. Undoubtedly he signed in order to maintain his throne and to limit the extent of the power he would relinquish.

52. **(J)** The United States Bill of Rights (the first ten amendments to the Constitution) is in no way related to the English "Bill of Rights." The United States document makes no mention of qualifications for voting. Rather, it sets forth specific rights and privileges offered to American citizens and to the individual states.

Test 4.   Natural Science Reading

1. **(C)** The migration of the lemmings appears to be purposeful. It consists of a relentless drive to the sea and an apparent urge to commit suicide. Many animals do form social groups of males from time to time, but these males do not permanently absent themselves from the company of females.

2. **(G)** The passage tells us that return migrations of insects are unknown, with the outstanding exception of the monarch butterfly.

3. **(B)** While the full influence of the reproductive instinct upon migration is not fully understood in most animals, it clearly is not a factor in the one-way migration of male lemmings. If anything, the factor operative with the lemmings is a self-destructive instinct.

4. **(F)** The migrations of caribou and locusts are motivated by the desire for better living conditions, specifically to search for food. Migration of salmon has to do with reproductive needs. None of the reasons suggested in the first paragraph seems to account for the behavior of lemmings.

5. **(C)** "Recent studies in the biochemistry of metabolism, showing that there is a seasonal cycle in the blood sugar (of birds) that has a definite relation to activity and food, seems to be among the most promising leads."

6. **(F)** The fourth paragraph explains the reproduction-linked migration of fish.

7. **(B)** Salmon live in the ocean, but at spawning time, they travel upstream to the freshwater rivers in which they were born. Golden plovers make an annual round trip between the Arctic and the tip of

South America. Locusts, lemmings, and honey bees are all one-way migrants.

8. **(H)** The passage tells us that return migrations in insects are rare. The exception to this generalization is the monarch butterfly, which is long-lived. The implication is that those animals that do not return migrate are short-lived.

9. **(C)** The purpose of this passage is to discuss migration and its various possible causes. The known facts are presented and various theories posited, with many questions raised but not answered.

10. **(G)** Since the migration of the lemmings occurs only in years when the population is very great, the migration of the adult males is evidently a means for reducing the size of the population, immediately and for the near future as well. This act could hardly be considered self-preservation, for the migrants perish, but controlling the population by this means is a form of species-preservation, for if the population were to grow unchecked, the food supply might be exhausted and all would perish.

11. **(D)** The migrations of the Lapps to the mountains in the summer and to the warmer valleys in the winter are based upon temperature and the availability of food supply, as are the migrations of caribou. In fact, the caribou is part of the food supply which the Lapps are following.

12. **(H)** San Juan Capistrano in southern California is the northern terminus of the swallows' migration. Their return there on the same date each year is governed by the same unknown factors that govern the very regular migrations of other birds—biochemistry, sex needs, length of days, etc.

13. **(A)** White light contains rays of all colors. If all the light hitting a piece of cloth is reflected, then all the color rays will also be reflected. We will see all the color rays together as white.

14. **(G)** We can see only colors whose rays are reflected; if no rays are reflected, we can see only the absence of color, which is black.

15. **(C)** The word *translucent* comes from the Latin and means *to shine through*. If light is neither absorbed nor reflected, it must shine through. A translucent object may also be transparent, but light shining through does not automatically denote transparency. The object may diffuse the light which passes through so that objects beyond cannot be clearly distinguished.

16. **(G)** If the tie, which reflects only red light, were to have no red light waves to reflect, it would absorb all other colors and appear to be black.

17. **(A)** We see objects only by the light that is reflected by them. An object perceived as black reflects no colors, but still reflects some light.

18. **(G)** Compensation is the process by which the eye and the brain accomodate for and neutralize the effects of artificial variations.

19. **(A)** The only entirely true statement is that artificial light is different from sunlight. Incandescent light contains more red and yellow than sunlight, but other types of artificial light, fluorescent for example, do not. The transparency of glass has to do with its manufacture and with the way light is passed through the glass; it has nothing to do with the nature of the light that shines upon it.

20. **(H)** Potassium nitrate is an ionic compound containing the potassium ion and the nitrate ion. In the solid state the ions are in a definite geometrical pattern forming the crystal.

21. **(B)** The loss of a neutron from the nucleus of an atom will decrease its atomic weight by one. The weight of an atom is a physical property. The atomic number is not the same as the atomic weight; it is based upon the number of protons in the atom. The chemical nature of an atom is influenced by the number of electrons, not the number of neutrons.

22. **(G)** $(NH_4)_2CrO_4$

$$
\begin{array}{llr}
\text{N:} & 2 \times 1 = & 2 \\
\text{H:} & 2 \times 4 = & 8 \\
\text{Cr:} & & 1 \\
\text{O:} & & \underline{4} \\
& & 15
\end{array}
$$

23. **(A)** A critical speed would be that speed at which the centrifugal force is equal to the gravitational force exerted on the block.

$$\frac{mv^2}{R} = mg$$
$$v = \sqrt{Rg}$$

24. **(G)** The cell vacuole is solely a storage compartment. A mitochondrion does contain a small amount of DNA.

25. **(B)** Living things belonging to the same species exhibit the ability to mate with one another, producing fertile offspring. This definition is applicable to most members of the same species. However, due to geographical isolation, many organisms have evolved separate and distinct methods of reproduction which may prevent them from mating with their counterparts found in other areas or locations. This variation on the species level has resulted in the formation of subspecies.

26. **(F)** A colloidal dispersion is composed of very small particles in a solvent. The solvent particles are larger than the molecular particles in a solution. Mineral oil is not a colloidal dispersion.

27. **(C)** Distillation is the process of separating soluble salts from a liquid by evaporating the liquid and then condensing it. Since the salt in seawater is in solution, it cannot be removed by filtration. Chlorination might serve to counter bacterial impurities in seawater, but would not reduce salinity.

28. **(G)** The volume of the acid times the normality of the acid is equal to the volume of the base times the normality of the base: $25(N) = (50)(.2)$. The normality of the acid = 0.4.

29. **(D)** All choices except (D) are members of the order *Mammalia*. The alligator is a reptile.

30. **(G)** The results approximate a 1:2:1 ratio which illustrates the genotypic ratio of Mendel's law of segregation. Aa × Aa results in 25 percent AA, 50 percent Aa, and 25 percent aa, the characteristic 1:2:1 ratio.

31. **(D)** Any material undergoing microscopic examination must be thin enough to enable light rays to pass through and be deflected upward through the body tube into the eyepiece. The finger, because of its thickness, is opaque.

32. **(F)** It is dangerous to taste an unknown substance; it may be poisonous.

33. **(C)** When sodium reacts with water, the gas produced is hydrogen. Hydrogen gas burns.

34. **(H)** Groups II and V had the same one-half hour of practice as Groups III and VI, but they had it massed in the first half hour, followed by distracting idleness of long duration.

35. **(A)** While the presentation of material to the subjects in Groups IV, V, and VI was audio-visual in nature, the actual learning procedure, the reading aloud of the syllables, was an instance of participatory or active learning.

36. **(F)** The groups which had been learning for a full hour were tired, and the experimenters did not want their results to be contaminated by fatigue.

37. **(D)** The most reasonable interpretation of these results is that distributed practice is more effective than massed practice.

38. **(F)** The most important control in this experiment was the use of subject matter that was unfamiliar to all subjects. Students rapidly invent mnemonic devices and devise private methods of learning, so that a true test of the efficacy of the two methods would have been impossible had students had previous experience with the type of material being learned.

39. **(C)** In light of the superiority of Groups IV, V, and VI, it is unlikely that subvocalization was an important factor in the learning of Groups I, II, and III. Had it been a factor, it might have influenced the results in ways unknown to the investigators.

40. **(G)** Nonsense syllables were the medium, not the object of this research. The investigators wanted to learn about the effects of massed and distributed practice and about the relative efficiency of private rote versus active learning.

41. **(D)** Since active participation in the learning process seems to produce more efficient learning, it follows that there should be greater results from more work in the science labs.

42. **(H)** One should not make a value judgment based on this experiment alone, but here active verbaliza-

tion of the connection between two members of a pair produced more efficient learning than passive learning of the pair as a given unit.

43. **(A)** Since the students who interrupted their study with short breaks performed best, we conclude that breaks are beneficial.

44. **(H)** Choice (H) is analogous to the conditions of Groups III and VI. (G) is analogous to the condition of Groups I and IV. (F) is analogous to the condition of Groups II and V.

45. **(C)** The death of the dinosaurs resulted from the same factors that determined the contours of the earth, namely changing temperatures, the movement of earth by ice caps, the rearrangement of land masses through the travel of continents, and to a lesser degree, erosion.

46. **(F)** *Tsunami* is the Japanese word for tidal wave. A typhoon is a hurricane that takes place in the Orient.

47. **(C)** A seismograph is an instrument that measures the intensity of earth tremors and earthquakes, expressed in degrees on the Richter scale.

48. **(G)** Eruptions of volcanos and geysers are each produced by the build-up of pressure deep in the earth and the subsequent release of this very hot material through a relatively small opening. While geysers erupt on a predictable and rhythmic schedule, volcanos are erratic.

49. **(C)** The eruption of a geyser releases hot water and steam.

50. **(F)** Naturally occurring earthquakes are caused by natural forces which are under study but which are so far not well understood. Those earthquakes caused by humans have been caused by the pressure of huge artificial lakes and by the pumping of water into holes bored deep into the earth.

51. **(C)** The author of this article appears wary lest we create major disasters with our new but uncontrolled technology. On the other hand, the author appears to be optimistic that with greater understanding of natural phenomena we may someday be able to control them and avert catastrophe.

52. **(G)** A tidal wave, despite its name, has nothing to do with tides, hence is not under the control of the moon. A naturally occurring tidal wave is the result of suboceanic earthquakes or massive shifts in the ocean floor. It travels across oceans with extreme speed, inundating land masses in its path.

ANSWER SHEET: MODEL SAT EXAM

Section I

1 Ⓐ Ⓑ Ⓒ Ⓓ Ⓔ	10 Ⓐ Ⓑ Ⓒ Ⓓ Ⓔ	19 Ⓐ Ⓑ Ⓒ Ⓓ Ⓔ	28 Ⓐ Ⓑ Ⓒ Ⓓ Ⓔ	37 Ⓐ Ⓑ Ⓒ Ⓓ Ⓔ
2 Ⓐ Ⓑ Ⓒ Ⓓ Ⓔ	11 Ⓐ Ⓑ Ⓒ Ⓓ Ⓔ	20 Ⓐ Ⓑ Ⓒ Ⓓ Ⓔ	29 Ⓐ Ⓑ Ⓒ Ⓓ Ⓔ	38 Ⓐ Ⓑ Ⓒ Ⓓ Ⓔ
3 Ⓐ Ⓑ Ⓒ Ⓓ Ⓔ	12 Ⓐ Ⓑ Ⓒ Ⓓ Ⓔ	21 Ⓐ Ⓑ Ⓒ Ⓓ Ⓔ	30 Ⓐ Ⓑ Ⓒ Ⓓ Ⓔ	39 Ⓐ Ⓑ Ⓒ Ⓓ Ⓔ
4 Ⓐ Ⓑ Ⓒ Ⓓ Ⓔ	13 Ⓐ Ⓑ Ⓒ Ⓓ Ⓔ	22 Ⓐ Ⓑ Ⓒ Ⓓ Ⓔ	31 Ⓐ Ⓑ Ⓒ Ⓓ Ⓔ	40 Ⓐ Ⓑ Ⓒ Ⓓ Ⓔ
5 Ⓐ Ⓑ Ⓒ Ⓓ Ⓔ	14 Ⓐ Ⓑ Ⓒ Ⓓ Ⓔ	23 Ⓐ Ⓑ Ⓒ Ⓓ Ⓔ	32 Ⓐ Ⓑ Ⓒ Ⓓ Ⓔ	41 Ⓐ Ⓑ Ⓒ Ⓓ Ⓔ
6 Ⓐ Ⓑ Ⓒ Ⓓ Ⓔ	15 Ⓐ Ⓑ Ⓒ Ⓓ Ⓔ	24 Ⓐ Ⓑ Ⓒ Ⓓ Ⓔ	33 Ⓐ Ⓑ Ⓒ Ⓓ Ⓔ	42 Ⓐ Ⓑ Ⓒ Ⓓ Ⓔ
7 Ⓐ Ⓑ Ⓒ Ⓓ Ⓔ	16 Ⓐ Ⓑ Ⓒ Ⓓ Ⓔ	25 Ⓐ Ⓑ Ⓒ Ⓓ Ⓔ	34 Ⓐ Ⓑ Ⓒ Ⓓ Ⓔ	43 Ⓐ Ⓑ Ⓒ Ⓓ Ⓔ
8 Ⓐ Ⓑ Ⓒ Ⓓ Ⓔ	17 Ⓐ Ⓑ Ⓒ Ⓓ Ⓔ	26 Ⓐ Ⓑ Ⓒ Ⓓ Ⓔ	35 Ⓐ Ⓑ Ⓒ Ⓓ Ⓔ	44 Ⓐ Ⓑ Ⓒ Ⓓ Ⓔ
9 Ⓐ Ⓑ Ⓒ Ⓓ Ⓔ	18 Ⓐ Ⓑ Ⓒ Ⓓ Ⓔ	27 Ⓐ Ⓑ Ⓒ Ⓓ Ⓔ	36 Ⓐ Ⓑ Ⓒ Ⓓ Ⓔ	45 Ⓐ Ⓑ Ⓒ Ⓓ Ⓔ

Section II

1 Ⓐ Ⓑ Ⓒ Ⓓ Ⓔ	6 Ⓐ Ⓑ Ⓒ Ⓓ Ⓔ	11 Ⓐ Ⓑ Ⓒ Ⓓ Ⓔ	16 Ⓐ Ⓑ Ⓒ Ⓓ Ⓔ	21 Ⓐ Ⓑ Ⓒ Ⓓ Ⓔ
2 Ⓐ Ⓑ Ⓒ Ⓓ Ⓔ	7 Ⓐ Ⓑ Ⓒ Ⓓ Ⓔ	12 Ⓐ Ⓑ Ⓒ Ⓓ Ⓔ	17 Ⓐ Ⓑ Ⓒ Ⓓ Ⓔ	22 Ⓐ Ⓑ Ⓒ Ⓓ Ⓔ
3 Ⓐ Ⓑ Ⓒ Ⓓ Ⓔ	8 Ⓐ Ⓑ Ⓒ Ⓓ Ⓔ	13 Ⓐ Ⓑ Ⓒ Ⓓ Ⓔ	18 Ⓐ Ⓑ Ⓒ Ⓓ Ⓔ	23 Ⓐ Ⓑ Ⓒ Ⓓ Ⓔ
4 Ⓐ Ⓑ Ⓒ Ⓓ Ⓔ	9 Ⓐ Ⓑ Ⓒ Ⓓ Ⓔ	14 Ⓐ Ⓑ Ⓒ Ⓓ Ⓔ	19 Ⓐ Ⓑ Ⓒ Ⓓ Ⓔ	24 Ⓐ Ⓑ Ⓒ Ⓓ Ⓔ
5 Ⓐ Ⓑ Ⓒ Ⓓ Ⓔ	10 Ⓐ Ⓑ Ⓒ Ⓓ Ⓔ	15 Ⓐ Ⓑ Ⓒ Ⓓ Ⓔ	20 Ⓐ Ⓑ Ⓒ Ⓓ Ⓔ	25 Ⓐ Ⓑ Ⓒ Ⓓ Ⓔ

Section III

1 Ⓐ Ⓑ Ⓒ Ⓓ Ⓔ	11 Ⓐ Ⓑ Ⓒ Ⓓ Ⓔ	21 Ⓐ Ⓑ Ⓒ Ⓓ Ⓔ	31 Ⓐ Ⓑ Ⓒ Ⓓ Ⓔ	41 Ⓐ Ⓑ Ⓒ Ⓓ Ⓔ
2 Ⓐ Ⓑ Ⓒ Ⓓ Ⓔ	12 Ⓐ Ⓑ Ⓒ Ⓓ Ⓔ	22 Ⓐ Ⓑ Ⓒ Ⓓ Ⓔ	32 Ⓐ Ⓑ Ⓒ Ⓓ Ⓔ	42 Ⓐ Ⓑ Ⓒ Ⓓ Ⓔ
3 Ⓐ Ⓑ Ⓒ Ⓓ Ⓔ	13 Ⓐ Ⓑ Ⓒ Ⓓ Ⓔ	23 Ⓐ Ⓑ Ⓒ Ⓓ Ⓔ	33 Ⓐ Ⓑ Ⓒ Ⓓ Ⓔ	43 Ⓐ Ⓑ Ⓒ Ⓓ Ⓔ
4 Ⓐ Ⓑ Ⓒ Ⓓ Ⓔ	14 Ⓐ Ⓑ Ⓒ Ⓓ Ⓔ	24 Ⓐ Ⓑ Ⓒ Ⓓ Ⓔ	34 Ⓐ Ⓑ Ⓒ Ⓓ Ⓔ	44 Ⓐ Ⓑ Ⓒ Ⓓ Ⓔ
5 Ⓐ Ⓑ Ⓒ Ⓓ Ⓔ	15 Ⓐ Ⓑ Ⓒ Ⓓ Ⓔ	25 Ⓐ Ⓑ Ⓒ Ⓓ Ⓔ	35 Ⓐ Ⓑ Ⓒ Ⓓ Ⓔ	45 Ⓐ Ⓑ Ⓒ Ⓓ Ⓔ
6 Ⓐ Ⓑ Ⓒ Ⓓ Ⓔ	16 Ⓐ Ⓑ Ⓒ Ⓓ Ⓔ	26 Ⓐ Ⓑ Ⓒ Ⓓ Ⓔ	36 Ⓐ Ⓑ Ⓒ Ⓓ Ⓔ	46 Ⓐ Ⓑ Ⓒ Ⓓ Ⓔ
7 Ⓐ Ⓑ Ⓒ Ⓓ Ⓔ	17 Ⓐ Ⓑ Ⓒ Ⓓ Ⓔ	27 Ⓐ Ⓑ Ⓒ Ⓓ Ⓔ	37 Ⓐ Ⓑ Ⓒ Ⓓ Ⓔ	47 Ⓐ Ⓑ Ⓒ Ⓓ Ⓔ
8 Ⓐ Ⓑ Ⓒ Ⓓ Ⓔ	18 Ⓐ Ⓑ Ⓒ Ⓓ Ⓔ	28 Ⓐ Ⓑ Ⓒ Ⓓ Ⓔ	38 Ⓐ Ⓑ Ⓒ Ⓓ Ⓔ	48 Ⓐ Ⓑ Ⓒ Ⓓ Ⓔ
9 Ⓐ Ⓑ Ⓒ Ⓓ Ⓔ	19 Ⓐ Ⓑ Ⓒ Ⓓ Ⓔ	29 Ⓐ Ⓑ Ⓒ Ⓓ Ⓔ	39 Ⓐ Ⓑ Ⓒ Ⓓ Ⓔ	49 Ⓐ Ⓑ Ⓒ Ⓓ Ⓔ
10 Ⓐ Ⓑ Ⓒ Ⓓ Ⓔ	20 Ⓐ Ⓑ Ⓒ Ⓓ Ⓔ	30 Ⓐ Ⓑ Ⓒ Ⓓ Ⓔ	40 Ⓐ Ⓑ Ⓒ Ⓓ Ⓔ	50 Ⓐ Ⓑ Ⓒ Ⓓ Ⓔ

Section IV

1 Ⓐ Ⓑ Ⓒ Ⓓ Ⓔ	8 Ⓐ Ⓑ Ⓒ Ⓓ Ⓔ	15 Ⓐ Ⓑ Ⓒ Ⓓ Ⓔ	22 Ⓐ Ⓑ Ⓒ Ⓓ Ⓔ	29 Ⓐ Ⓑ Ⓒ Ⓓ Ⓔ
2 Ⓐ Ⓑ Ⓒ Ⓓ Ⓔ	9 Ⓐ Ⓑ Ⓒ Ⓓ Ⓔ	16 Ⓐ Ⓑ Ⓒ Ⓓ Ⓔ	23 Ⓐ Ⓑ Ⓒ Ⓓ Ⓔ	30 Ⓐ Ⓑ Ⓒ Ⓓ Ⓔ
3 Ⓐ Ⓑ Ⓒ Ⓓ Ⓔ	10 Ⓐ Ⓑ Ⓒ Ⓓ Ⓔ	17 Ⓐ Ⓑ Ⓒ Ⓓ Ⓔ	24 Ⓐ Ⓑ Ⓒ Ⓓ Ⓔ	31 Ⓐ Ⓑ Ⓒ Ⓓ Ⓔ
4 Ⓐ Ⓑ Ⓒ Ⓓ Ⓔ	11 Ⓐ Ⓑ Ⓒ Ⓓ Ⓔ	18 Ⓐ Ⓑ Ⓒ Ⓓ Ⓔ	25 Ⓐ Ⓑ Ⓒ Ⓓ Ⓔ	32 Ⓐ Ⓑ Ⓒ Ⓓ Ⓔ
5 Ⓐ Ⓑ Ⓒ Ⓓ Ⓔ	12 Ⓐ Ⓑ Ⓒ Ⓓ Ⓔ	19 Ⓐ Ⓑ Ⓒ Ⓓ Ⓔ	26 Ⓐ Ⓑ Ⓒ Ⓓ Ⓔ	33 Ⓐ Ⓑ Ⓒ Ⓓ Ⓔ
6 Ⓐ Ⓑ Ⓒ Ⓓ Ⓔ	13 Ⓐ Ⓑ Ⓒ Ⓓ Ⓔ	20 Ⓐ Ⓑ Ⓒ Ⓓ Ⓔ	27 Ⓐ Ⓑ Ⓒ Ⓓ Ⓔ	34 Ⓐ Ⓑ Ⓒ Ⓓ Ⓔ
7 Ⓐ Ⓑ Ⓒ Ⓓ Ⓔ	14 Ⓐ Ⓑ Ⓒ Ⓓ Ⓔ	21 Ⓐ Ⓑ Ⓒ Ⓓ Ⓔ	28 Ⓐ Ⓑ Ⓒ Ⓓ Ⓔ	35 Ⓐ Ⓑ Ⓒ Ⓓ Ⓔ

Section V

1 Ⓐ Ⓑ Ⓒ Ⓓ Ⓔ	9 Ⓐ Ⓑ Ⓒ Ⓓ Ⓔ	17 Ⓐ Ⓑ Ⓒ Ⓓ Ⓔ	25 Ⓐ Ⓑ Ⓒ Ⓓ Ⓔ	33 Ⓐ Ⓑ Ⓒ Ⓓ Ⓔ
2 Ⓐ Ⓑ Ⓒ Ⓓ Ⓔ	10 Ⓐ Ⓑ Ⓒ Ⓓ Ⓔ	18 Ⓐ Ⓑ Ⓒ Ⓓ Ⓔ	26 Ⓐ Ⓑ Ⓒ Ⓓ Ⓔ	34 Ⓐ Ⓑ Ⓒ Ⓓ Ⓔ
3 Ⓐ Ⓑ Ⓒ Ⓓ Ⓔ	11 Ⓐ Ⓑ Ⓒ Ⓓ Ⓔ	19 Ⓐ Ⓑ Ⓒ Ⓓ Ⓔ	27 Ⓐ Ⓑ Ⓒ Ⓓ Ⓔ	35 Ⓐ Ⓑ Ⓒ Ⓓ Ⓔ
4 Ⓐ Ⓑ Ⓒ Ⓓ Ⓔ	12 Ⓐ Ⓑ Ⓒ Ⓓ Ⓔ	20 Ⓐ Ⓑ Ⓒ Ⓓ Ⓔ	28 Ⓐ Ⓑ Ⓒ Ⓓ Ⓔ	36 Ⓐ Ⓑ Ⓒ Ⓓ Ⓔ
5 Ⓐ Ⓑ Ⓒ Ⓓ Ⓔ	13 Ⓐ Ⓑ Ⓒ Ⓓ Ⓔ	21 Ⓐ Ⓑ Ⓒ Ⓓ Ⓔ	29 Ⓐ Ⓑ Ⓒ Ⓓ Ⓔ	37 Ⓐ Ⓑ Ⓒ Ⓓ Ⓔ
6 Ⓐ Ⓑ Ⓒ Ⓓ Ⓔ	14 Ⓐ Ⓑ Ⓒ Ⓓ Ⓔ	22 Ⓐ Ⓑ Ⓒ Ⓓ Ⓔ	30 Ⓐ Ⓑ Ⓒ Ⓓ Ⓔ	38 Ⓐ Ⓑ Ⓒ Ⓓ Ⓔ
7 Ⓐ Ⓑ Ⓒ Ⓓ Ⓔ	15 Ⓐ Ⓑ Ⓒ Ⓓ Ⓔ	23 Ⓐ Ⓑ Ⓒ Ⓓ Ⓔ	31 Ⓐ Ⓑ Ⓒ Ⓓ Ⓔ	39 Ⓐ Ⓑ Ⓒ Ⓓ Ⓔ
8 Ⓐ Ⓑ Ⓒ Ⓓ Ⓔ	16 Ⓐ Ⓑ Ⓒ Ⓓ Ⓔ	24 Ⓐ Ⓑ Ⓒ Ⓓ Ⓔ	32 Ⓐ Ⓑ Ⓒ Ⓓ Ⓔ	40 Ⓐ Ⓑ Ⓒ Ⓓ Ⓔ

SECTION I: VERBAL ABILITIES

45 Questions
Time—30 Minutes

Directions: Each of the following items contains a word in capital letters, followed by five words or phrases. Select the word or phrase most nearly *opposite* in meaning to the capitalized word.

1. MINIMIZE :
   - (A) endanger
   - (B) list
   - (C) destroy
   - (D) expand
   - (E) itemize

2. MONOTONOUS :
   - (A) muddled
   - (B) incomprehensible
   - (C) exciting
   - (D) acceptable
   - (E) difficult

3. INNOVATE :
   - (A) buy
   - (B) sell
   - (C) own
   - (D) copy
   - (E) choose

4. OMNIPOTENT :
   - (A) healthy
   - (B) safe
   - (C) good
   - (D) weak
   - (E) sour

5. AMATEUR :
   - (A) dabbler
   - (B) professional
   - (C) expert
   - (D) skillful
   - (E) trustworthy

6. DOWNFALL :
   - (A) harm
   - (B) hazard
   - (C) weakness
   - (D) success
   - (E) quiet

7. EULOGIZE :
   - (A) honor
   - (B) ignore
   - (C) defend
   - (D) berate
   - (E) heal

.8. TURGID :
   - (A) dusty
   - (B) muddy
   - (C) rolling
   - (D) deflated
   - (E) tense

9. EXPUNGE :
   - (A) clarify
   - (B) cleanse
   - (C) perpetuate
   - (D) investigate
   - (E) underline

10. IGNOMINY :
   - (A) fame
   - (B) isolation
   - (C) misfortune
   - (D) sorrow
   - (E) stupidity

11. RELEVANT :

    (A) ingenious
    (B) inspiring
    (C) obvious
    (D) inappropriate
    (E) tentative

12. DISPARAGE :

    (A) applaud
    (B) degrade
    (C) erase
    (D) reform
    (E) scatter

13. OPULENT :

    (A) fearful
    (B) free
    (C) oversized
    (D) trustful
    (E) impoverished

14. PROPITIATE :

    (A) anger
    (B) approach
    (C) predict
    (D) applaud
    (E) promote

15. DEVIOUS :

    (A) candid
    (B) clever
    (C) bright
    (D) bitter
    (E) vane

Directions: Each of the following sentences contains one or two blank spaces to be filled in by one of the five choices listed below each sentence. Select the word or words that *best* complete the meaning of the sentence.

16. They acted in concert, each _____ for a(n) _____ of the plot.

    (A) reliable—source
    (B) responsible—element
    (C) unavailable—section
    (D) appointed—article
    (E) agreeable—felony

17. They were unwisely _____ during their education, and _____ was the result.

    (A) neglected—ignorance
    (B) interrupted—consistency
    (C) befriended—alienation

    (D) instructed—genius
    (E) taught—attendance

18. Communist countries have denied the _____ of capitalist ones for many years, _____ success of suppressing it.

    (A) economy—regretting
    (B) rhetoric—without
    (C) supremacy—negotiating
    (D) vision—admitting
    (E) decline—boasting

19. _____ his duties as an officer of the law, the policeman _____ the prisoner.

    (A) Inflating—eschewed
    (B) Displaying—retired
    (C) Announcing—reversed
    (D) Forgetting—released
    (E) Renouncing—fed

20. Profit-minded top-level management decided to _____ operations in _____ market areas.

    (A) curtail—solid
    (B) influence—unimportant
    (C) improve—unattended
    (D) reduce—promising
    (E) increase—helpless

Directions: Each of the following reading passages is followed by a set of questions. Read each passage and answer the accompanying questions, basing your answers on what is *stated* or *implied* in the passage.

French portrait painting in the years immediately following the French Revolution developed a character all its own. The bitter experience of the Revolution created a people who had lost their ability to idealize, and could only recognize a reality they could see. Naturalism became a jealous god that purged completely the elements of Romanticism—be they classical, Walterian, Bolati, or whatever—with which it had found a certain compatibility in the first half of the century. We can see naturalism as an end in itself in the late portraits of Francis Peters, where the earlier Walterian ideal was swept aside. It can also be seen in the work of James Ellis Green, whose portrait of General Lefete is no match for his marvelous equestrian "Welton." And it can be recognized in countless other painters of the period. It has gained for the sixties and seventies the reputation of an art that is crass and banal in its naturalism, devoid of any poetry. With some justification, the question has been asked whether a painter that was so captivated by objectivism and the pursuit of reality could attain the level of the highest form of art. The painted portrait in America experienced the same disastrous result. An excessive naturalism had been encouraged by the appearance of the camera, which produced an image of total objectivity and accuracy, and unfortunately both patron and artist accepted this as the true form of art. The photographic naturalism of the painted portrait was not to be outdone by the modeled portrait, and American portraiture had to await the arrival of such men as Jerome Singer, John Elkin, and Jerode Balter to restore Art with a capital A upon the throne usurped by Naturalism with a capital N. To rise above the dull mediocrity it had achieved, naturalism had to be revitalized with elegance and heroism.

21. According to the author, after the French Revolution French portrait painting

    (A) was returned to the common man
    (B) improved its idealism
    (C) decreased in quality
    (D) developed into a modern classicism
    (E) returned to Romanticism

22. Each of the following is mentioned as affecting art in the 1870s *except*

    (A) photography
    (B) war
    (C) objectivism
    (D) naturalism
    (E) religion

23. It seems to be that the thing the author dislikes most about the art following the French Revolution is its

    (A) inability to make changes
    (B) use of naturalism
    (C) poor craftsmanship
    (D) lack of elegance
    (E) poor choice of subject matter

24. The author implies that he liked least the works of

    (A) Green
    (B) Singer
    (C) Peters
    (D) Bolati
    (E) Walter

25. The article's main purpose is to

    (A) discuss the reasons for the changes in some of the art of the mid-1800s
    (B) show how war can destroy art
    (C) urge that art take a turn from naturalism
    (D) show how classical art and modern art are alike
    (E) explain the unpopularity of the art of the mid-1880s

The first reaction one has to the question of viable approaches to the control of chemical and biological weapons is that there are no such approaches. And it is most difficult to dispense with this first reaction. The reasons are that the nations, including some of the smaller ones, are already downstream too far. The larger arsenals for CB warfare may be restricted to the major powers, but there is little doubt that an increasing capability is proliferating in some of the smaller and developing countries. What used to be largely a picture of research has turned to development, and development has turned to manufacturing and stockpiling. The subject is shrouded in secrecy and it is the secrecy which seems to provide a non-stop momentum to realize the full potential of these types of weapons. No one really knows what someone else may have ready for employment in a military situation. The large and expensive programs in the United States and the Soviet Union are attributed to each other's "large and expensive programs." Knowledge and capability required for detection and defense are tied to knowledge and capability for retaliation. The "no first use" policy of the United States and other major nations implies that this retaliation be in kind, and this requires that weapons of the CB class be available.

A philosophy of mutual deterrence is developing in CB warfare comparable to that in nuclear warfare. In fact, much of the literature on the subject repeats that the stalemate in the latter opens up the need for capability in the former. As an arms race, CBW does not present the spiraling costs of the ICBM–ABM systems, hence a movement to CB weapons (especially chemical) among some smaller nations. So far as the major powers are concerned, the elements in CBW which are in common with the nuclear arms race include the now-accepted approach to that race. Thus in discussing control of CB warfare, an editorial in the British journal, *Nature*, concluded:

"The balance of terror between the great power

blocs may not be to everybody's taste, but it is probably still the best way of avoiding war.''

26. It can be inferred that the control of chemical and biological warfare

    (A) is less costly than controlling other systems of warfare
    (B) may not be possible or necessarily desirable
    (C) is in the hands of the United States and Russia
    (D) should become a matter of prime importance
    (E) is necessary before small nations become involved

27. Which of the following is not given as a cause for the continued development of CB weapons?

    (A) increased hostilities between the nations involved
    (B) the need to have CB weapons with which to retaliate
    (C) the need to be able to detect a CB attack
    (D) other weapons programs are more costly than the development of a CB system
    (E) the countries involved are unaware of what the others are doing

28. The writer in the British journal might feel that the research and development of CB systems should be

    (A) encouraged and expanded
    (B) conducted only by the major powers
    (C) immediately halted
    (D) maintained as it is now
    (E) considered necessary and desirable

29. The justification for the United States' participation in CB warfare programs is mainly due to the

    (A) need for undetectable weaponry
    (B) still untapped knowledge in that field
    (C) costliness of the nuclear programs
    (D) Soviet Union's having such a program
    (E) ability of modern research to develop them

30. The main purpose of this article is to

    (A) show the difficulties involved in stopping CB warfare programs

    (B) explain the cost of CB warfare
    (C) discuss alternatives to CB warfare
    (D) chronicle the history of CB warfare
    (E) make the reader aware of the dangers of CB warfare

Directions: Select the word or set of words that *best* complete each of the following sentences.

31. With _____ faith, the members of the parish attended church morning and evening like so many others in the area.

    (A) incomparable
    (B) unwavering
    (C) unusual
    (D) unregimented
    (E) unlikely

32. Changing his mind with every new development, the governor gave the appearance of being _____ .

    (A) unequivocal
    (B) self-reliant
    (C) unfinished
    (D) reliable
    (E) unsteady

33. She thought her city the most unattractive of the three cities: most congested, most polluted, most _____ .

    (A) unlivable
    (B) fatal
    (C) cosmopolitan
    (D) delineated
    (E) empty

34. The _____ of the final examination could not compensate for the pressure it had brought the students.

    (A) valor
    (B) importance
    (C) power
    (D) ease
    (E) stipend

35. He was confused about the outcome of his case and called his attorney to _____ it.

    (A) contest
    (B) dismiss
    (C) fulfill

(D) recommend
(E) discuss

Directions: Each of the following items contains a pair of words in capital letters, followed by five pairs of words. Choose the pair that *best* expresses a relationship similar to the one expressed by the capitalized pair.

36. AWL : PUNCTURE ::

   (A) tire : flat
   (B) cleaver : cut
   (C) plane : area
   (D) throttle : gas
   (E) axle : wheel

37. LUSH : BARREN ::

   (A) delicious : appetite
   (B) drunk : stupid
   (C) jungle : desert
   (D) hot : cold
   (E) obvious : plain

38. CURVED : GNARLED ::

   (A) twisted : bent
   (B) ripple : wavy
   (C) silent : noise
   (D) stiff : inflexible
   (E) tire : top

39. REVOLVE : SPIN ::

   (A) move : travel
   (B) comfortable : dizzy
   (C) turn : twisted
   (D) ride : whirl
   (E) tire : top

40. AIR : STAGNATE ::

   (A) rust : iron
   (B) water : odor
   (C) wood : rot
   (D) fish : spoiled
   (E) animal : die

41. MUNIFICENT : GENEROUS ::

   (A) dolorous : sorrowful
   (B) domineering : retiring
   (C) indisputable : doubtful
   (D) hapless : fortunate
   (E) beguiled : judicious

42. SCIENTIST : LABORATORY ::

   (A) chemist : test tube
   (B) lawyer : client
   (C) dentist : drill
   (D) teacher : classroom
   (E) actor : playwright

43. PROGRAM : COMPUTER ::

   (A) student : book
   (B) conference : meeting
   (C) recipe : cook
   (D) index : book
   (E) picture : photograph

44. JOCULAR : SOLEMN ::

   (A) latent : perceptible
   (B) pomp : spectacle
   (C) raze : destroy
   (D) vindictive : vengeful
   (E) solo : one

45. STOCKHOLDER : DIVIDENDS ::

   (A) stockbroker : tickertape
   (B) banker : lend
   (C) president : congress
   (D) dollars : monies
   (E) songwriter : royalties

STOP

END OF SECTION I. IF YOU HAVE ANY TIME LEFT,
GO OVER YOUR WORK IN THIS SECTION ONLY. DO
NOT WORK IN ANY OTHER SECTION OF THE TEST.

SECTION II: MATHEMATICAL ABILITIES

25 Questions
Time—30 Minutes

Directions: The following problems are to be solved using any available space on the page for scratchwork. When a problem has been worked out, mark your answer on the answer sheet.

The following information should be helpful in determining the correct answers for some of the problems:

Circle of radius r: Area = πr^2; Circumference = $2\pi r$. The number of degrees of an arc in a circle is 360. The measure of degrees of a straight angle is 180.

Definitions of symbols:

∥ is parallel to	> is greater than
≦ is less than or equal to	< is less than
≧ is greater than or equal to	⊥ is perpendicular to
∠ angle	△ triangle

Triangle: The sum of the measures in degrees of the angles is 180. The angle BDC is a right angle; therefore,

(1) the area of triangle ABC = $\dfrac{AC \times BD}{2}$

(2) $AB^2 = AD^2 + DB^2$

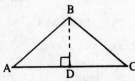

Note: The figures accompanying the problems are drawn as accurately as possible unless otherwise stated in specific problems. Again, unless otherwise stated, all figures lie in the same plane. All numbers used in these problems are real numbers.

1. The ice compartment in a refrigerator is 8 inches deep, 5 inches high, and 4 inches wide. How many ice cubes will it hold if each cube is 2 inches on each edge?

   (A) 16
   (B) 20
   (C) 24
   (D) 80
   (E) 160

2. QOR is a quadrant of a circle. PS = 6 and PT = 8. What is the length of arc QR?

   (A) 10π
   (B) 5π
   (C) 20π

(D) 24
(E) cannot be determined from the information given

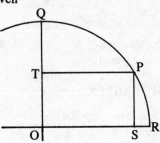

3. In the figure, line PQ is parallel to line RS, angle y = 60°, and angle z = 130°. How many degrees are there in angle x?

   (A) 90°
   (B) 100°
   (C) 110°
   (D) 120°
   (E) 130°

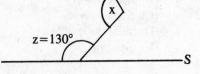

4. If for all real numbers (a.b.c. − d.e.f.) = (a−d) × (b−e) × (c−f) then (4.5.6. − 1.2.3.) =

   (A) −27
   (B) 0
   (C) 27
   (D) 54
   (E) 108

5. PQRS is a square and PTS is an equilateral triangle. How many degrees are there in angle TRS?

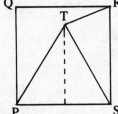

   (A) 60
   (B) 75
   (C) 80
   (D) 50
   (E) cannot be determined from the information given

114

6. Under certain conditions, sound travels at about 1,100 ft. per second. If 88 ft. per second is approximately equivalent to 60 miles per hour, the speed of sound under the above conditions is closest to

   (A) 730 miles per hour
   (B) 740 miles per hour
   (C) 750 miles per hour
   (D) 760 miles per hour
   (E) 780 miles per hour

7. The sum of an odd number and an even number is

   (A) sometimes an even number
   (B) always divisible by 3 or 5 or 7
   (C) always an odd number
   (D) always a prime number (not divisible)
   (E) always divisible by 2

8. If one angle of a triangle is three times a second angle and the third angle is 20 degrees more than the second angle, the second angle, in degrees, is

   (A) 64
   (B) 34
   (C) 40
   (D) 50
   (E) 32

9. If on a blueprint ¼ inch equals 12 inches, what is the actual length in feet of a steel bar that is represented on the blueprint by a line 3⅜ inches long?

   (A) 3⅜
   (B) 6¾
   (C) 2½
   (D) 13½
   (E) 9

10. A square root has a diagonal of x units. If the diagonal is increased by 2 units, what is the length of the side of the new square?

    (A) $x + 2$
    (B) $(x + 2)\sqrt{2}$
    (C) $\dfrac{(x + 2)\sqrt{2}}{2}$
    (D) $(x + 2)2$
    (E) $\dfrac{(x + 2)\sqrt{2}}{4}$

11. A math class has 27 students in it. Of those students 14 are also enrolled in history and 17 are enrolled in English. What is the minimum percentage of the students in the math class who are also enrolled in history *and* English?

    (A) 15%
    (B) 22%
    (C) 49%
    (D) 63%
    (E) 91%

12. A cylindrical container has a diameter of 14 inches and a height of 6 inches. Since one gallon equals 231 cubic inches, the capacity of the tank is approximately

    (A) 2²/₇ gallons
    (B) 4 gallons
    (C) 1¹/₇ gallons
    (D) ⅔ gallon
    (E) 2⅔ gallons

13. A train running between two towns arrives at its destination 10 minutes late when it goes 40 miles per hour and 16 minutes late when it goes 30 miles per hour. The distance between the towns is

    (A) 720 miles
    (B) 12 miles
    (C) 8⁶/₇ miles
    (D) 192 miles
    (E) 560 miles

14. If Paul can paint a fence in 2 hours and Fred can paint the same fence in 3 hours, Paul and Fred working together can paint the fence in

    (A) 2.5 hours
    (B) ⁵/₆ hour
    (C) 5 hours
    (D) 1 hour
    (E) 1.2 hours

15. A motorist drives 60 miles to her destination at an average speed of 40 miles per hour and makes the return trip at an average rate of 30 miles per hour. Her average speed per hour for the entire trip is

    (A) 35 miles
    (B) 70 miles
    (C) 43⅓ miles

(D) 17 miles

(E) 34²/₇ miles

16. The number of grams in one ounce is 28.35. The number of grams in a kilogram is 1000. Therefore, the number of kilograms in one pound is approximately

(A) 2.2

(B) 1.0

(C) 0.045

(D) 4.5

(E) 0.45

17. If one third of the liquid contents of a can evaporates on the first day and three fourths of the remainder evaporates on the second day, the fractional part of the original contents remaining at the close of the second day is

(A) ⁵/₁₂

(B) ⁷/₁₂

(C) ⅙

(D) ½

(E) ¼

18. If n and d represent positive whole numbers (n > d > 1), the fractions

I. $\frac{d}{n}$ II. $\frac{d+1}{n+1}$ III. $\frac{d-1}{n-1}$

IV. $\frac{n}{d}$ V. $\frac{n-1}{d-1}$

arranged in ascending order of magnitude, are represented correctly by

(A) III, II, I, V, IV

(B) IV, V, III, I, II

(C) II, I, IV, III, V

(D) III, V, IV, I, II

(E) III, I, II, IV, V

19. The formula for the selling price S of an article sold at a loss of r% of its cost C is

(A) $S = C(1 - r)$

(B) $S = \frac{C(1 - r)}{10}$

(C) $S = \frac{C(1 - r)}{100}$

(D) $S = 100C(1 - r)$

(E) $S = \frac{C(100 - r)}{100}$

20. Three circles share a common center, point O. The smallest circle has a radius of 2, the next circle a radius of 5, and the largest circle a radius of 9. What fraction of the area of the largest circle is the area of the shaded region?

(A) ⅓

(B) ⁷/₂₇

(C) ²⁵/₈₁

(D) ⁷/₁₁

(E) ¹²/₁₇

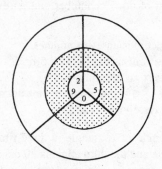

21. If x is a fraction which ranges from ¼ to ½ and y is a fraction which ranges from ¾ to ¹¹/₁₂, what is the maximum value for $^x/_y$?

(A) ¹¹/₄₈

(B) ¹¹/₂₄

(C) ³/₁₆

(D) ⅜

(E) ⅔

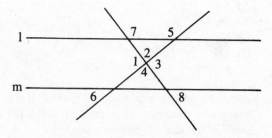

22. In the figure above, which of the following must be equal to 180 degrees?

I. 1 plus 3

II. 2 plus 4

III. 5 plus 6

IV. 7 plus 8

V. 8 plus 6

(A) I and II only
(B) III and IV only
(C) V only
(D) I, II, III, IV only
(E) I, II, III, IV, V

23. Which one of the following numbers is not a perfect square?

(A) .16
(B) 1.6
(C) 16
(D) 1,600
(E) .0016

24. If $x = \frac{3}{2}$ and $y = 2$, then $x + y^2 - \frac{1}{2} =$

(A) 5
(B) 10
(C) 11½
(D) 9½
(E) $\frac{6}{2}$

25. If $6x + 12 = 9$, $|x| =$

(A) $\frac{21}{6}$
(B) $-\frac{1}{2}$
(C) $\frac{9}{12}$
(D) ½
(E) $\frac{9}{6}$

STOP

END OF SECTION II. IF YOU HAVE ANY TIME LEFT, GO OVER YOUR WORK IN THIS SECTION ONLY. DO NOT WORK IN ANY OTHER SECTION OF THE TEST.

SECTION III: TEST OF STANDARD WRITTEN ENGLISH

50 Questions
Time—30 Minutes

Directions: The sentences below contain errors in grammar, usage, word choice, and idiom. Parts of each sentence are underlined and lettered. Decide which underlined part contains the error and mark its letter on your answer sheet. If the sentence is correct as it stands, mark (E) on your answer sheet. No sentence contains more than one error.

1. The evidence of their tombs suggest that the
   A
   ancient Egyptians believed that each man could
   B
   provide for his own happy afterlife. No error.
   C   D   E

2. She gathered up all the apples and, putting them
   A   B
   in a basket, carries them into the house. No
   C   D   E
   error.

3. His grandfather was one of the millions of immigrants fleeing eastern Europe which landed
   A   B   C
   at Ellis Island during the early years of this cen-
   D
   tury. No error.
   E

4. There was a time when the Arctic was unknown
   A
   territory; now, scientists are manning research
   B
   stations there and to gather data on the frozen
   C   D
   region. No error.
   E

5. Mary was so disinterested in the baseball game
   A   B
   that she yawned unashamedly. No error.
   C   D   E

6. Nigeria, a former British colony and protecto-
   A   B
   rate, it gained its independence and became a
   C   D
   member of the British Commonwealth of Nations. No error.
   E

7. One of the cornerstones of modern physics, the
   A
   principle of the conservation of energy was for-
   B   C   D
   mulated by Leibnitz in the seventeenth century.

   No error.
   E

8. Tuck a dish towel over the potatoes to keep
   A   B
   them warm and to absorb steam so that they
   C
   will not become soggily. No error.
   D   E

9. A round and white sun emblazoned at the sum-
   A   B   C
   mit of the sky. No error.
   D   E

10. When the members of a committee are so at
    A B
    odds that they are on the verge of offering their
    C
    resignations, problems become insoluble. No
    D   E
    error.

11. One of the requirements was a course in English
    A   B   C
    literature of the sixteenth centuries. No error.
    D   E

118

12. Each one of us <u>have</u> <u>looked over</u> <u>his</u> own part,
                 A   B   C
    but we haven't rehearsed together <u>yet</u>. <u>No error</u>.
                                    D   E

13. <u>Further</u> acquaintance with the <u>memoirs</u> of Eliz-
      A   B
    abeth Barrett Browning and Robert Browning

    <u>enable</u> us to appreciate the degree of influence
     C
    that two people of talent can have <u>on</u> each other.
                                       D
    <u>No error</u>.
     E

14. When my <u>commanding</u> officer first <u>looked up</u>
                A   B
    <u>from</u> his desk, he <u>took</u> Lieutenant Baxter to be
     A   C
    <u>I</u>. <u>No error</u>.
     D   E

15. Though he <u>had awakened</u> before the birds began
                 A
    to <u>twitter</u>, he <u>laid</u> in bed until long after the sun
      B   C
    <u>had arisen</u>. <u>No error</u>.
      D   E

16. As she <u>dived</u> off the springboard, she was <u>hor</u>-
          A   B
    <u>rified</u> to see that the water <u>was drained</u> from the
                              C
    pool the night <u>before</u>. <u>No error</u>.
                  D   E

17. The ceremonies <u>were opened</u> by a drum and
                    A
    bugle <u>corps</u> of Chinese <u>school</u> children <u>parading</u>
         B   C   D
    up the street in colorful uniforms. <u>No error</u>.
                                       E

18. <u>Irregardless</u> of <u>what</u> other members of the board
        A   B
    say, as <u>chairperson</u> I must repeat that these are
            C
    the facts <u>concerning</u> the requirements for the
               D
    position. <u>No error</u>.
             E

19. There <u>would have been</u> no objections to <u>him</u>
               A   B
    joining the party if he <u>had been</u> <u>amenable</u> to the
                            C   D
    plans of the group. <u>No error</u>.
                        E

20. <u>Five-year-old</u> Joanne, in her <u>naiveté</u>, explained
     A   B
    her absence from school with an <u>incredulous</u>
                                  C
    tale <u>in which</u> she played the role of the daring
         D
    heroine. <u>No error</u>.
             E

21. While the organ <u>sounded</u> a <u>solemn</u> march,
                   A   B
    <u>slowly</u> the mourners <u>past</u> through the doors of
     C   D
    the church. <u>No error</u>.
                  E

22. Jack <u>likes</u> <u>all</u> sports: tennis, basketball, <u>football</u>,
         A   B   C
    and etc. <u>No error</u>.
      D   E

23. That <u>Bill's</u> reasoning was <u>fallacious</u> was soon
     A B   C
    apparent <u>to all</u>. <u>No error</u>.
          D   E

24. Neither John <u>nor</u> his children <u>is</u> likely to attend
     A   B   C
    the <u>ceremonies</u>. <u>No error</u>.
         D   E

25. He will give the <u>message</u> to <u>whoever</u> <u>opens</u> the
             A   B   C   D
    door. <u>No error</u>.
         E

Directions: The following sentences contain problems in grammar, sentence construction, word choice, and punctuation. Part or all of each sentence is underlined. Select the lettered answer that contains the best version of the underlined section. Answer (A) always repeats the original underlined section exactly. If the sentence is correct as it stands, select (A).

26. Both <u>being overweight and to smoke cigarettes increase one's chances</u> of suffering some form of heart disease.

    (A) being overweight and to smoke cigarettes increase one's chances
    (B) being overweight and to smoke cigarettes increases one's chances
    (C) to be overweight and the smoking of cigarettes increase one's chances
    (D) being overweight and smoking cigarettes increase one's chances
    (E) being overweight and to smoke cigarettes increase ones chances

27. We can't do their job since <u>its difficult to do even ours</u>.

    (A) its difficult to do even ours
    (B) its difficult to do even our's
    (C) its' difficult to do even ours'
    (D) it's difficult to do even ours
    (E) its difficult to do ours even

28. She insisted <u>on me going</u>.

    (A) on me going
    (B) on I going
    (C) for me to go
    (D) upon me going
    (E) on my going

29. <u>If the parent would have shown more interest,</u> her daughter would have been in college today.

    (A) If the parent would have shown more interest,
    (B) If the parent had shown more interest,
    (C) If the parent would have showed more interest,
    (D) If the parent would have been showing more interest,
    (E) Should the parent have shown more interest,

30. Information recorded by the Voyager I spacecraft indicated that Jupiter has <u>an aurora borealis similar to earth's and a surface</u> covered with swirling gases.

    (A) an aurora borealis similar to earth's and a surface
    (B) an aurora borealis similar to earth and a surface
    (C) an aurora borealis similar to earth's and it's surface
    (D) an aurora borealis similarly to earth's and a surface
    (E) an aurora borealis which is like to earth's and a surface

31. <u>She never has and she never will do any work.</u>

    (A) She never has and she never will do any work.
    (B) She never has and she never will do no work.
    (C) She never has, and she never will do any work.
    (D) Never has she and never will she do any work.
    (E) She never has done and she never will do any work.

32. <u>By means of using a new live-virus vaccine,</u> Swiss scientists hope to reduce the incidence of rabies among foxes in Europe.

    (A) By means of using a new live-virus vaccine,
    (B) By means of a new live-virus vaccine being used,
    (C) Using a new live-virus vaccine,
    (D) By means of using a new live-virus vaccine.
    (E) By means of using a new live-virus vaccine;

33. <u>Interviewed for a magazine article on television, violence in children's programs was condemned by some parents.</u>

    (A) Interviewed for a magazine article on television, violence in children's programs was condemned by some parents.
    (B) Violence in children's programs was condemned by some parents interviewed for a magazine article on television.
    (C) Interviewed for a magazine article on television, violence in children's programings was condemned by some parents.
    (D) Interviewed for a magazine article on television, children's programs' violence was condemned by some parents.
    (E) Interviewed for a magazine article on television, violent children's programs were condemned by some parents.

34. <u>He supposed me to be him.</u>

    (A) He supposed me to be him.
    (B) He supposed me to be he.
    (C) He supposed I to be him.
    (D) He supposed l to be he.
    (E) He thought me to be he.

35. <u>Being as it is an underdeveloped country,</u> Laos has no railroads and few highways.

    (A) Being as it is an underdeveloped country,
    (B) Due to it being an underdeveloped country,
    (C) Seeing as how it is an underdeveloped country,
    (D) An underdeveloped country,
    (E) With the country being underdeveloped,

36. <u>Everyone, including Anne and Helen, were there.</u>

    (A) Everyone, including Anne and Helen, were there.
    (B) Everyone including Anne and Helen, were there.
    (C) Everyone, including Anne and Helen, was there.
    (D) Everyone, including Anne, and Helen, were there.
    (E) Everyone including Anne and Helen were there.

37. Charles would <u>rather ski than to play tennis.</u>

    (A) rather ski than to play tennis
    (B) rather skiing than to play tennis
    (C) rather ski then to play tennis
    (D) find skiing to be preferable to playing tennis
    (E) rather ski than play tennis

38. I was very excited <u>at the news, that's why</u> I dropped the groceries.

    (A) at the news, that's why
    (B) by the news, that's why
    (C) at the news; that's why
    (D) at the news, that is why
    (E) at the news that's why

39. The reason I plan to go is <u>because she will be disappointed</u> if I don't.

    (A) because she will be disappointed
    (B) that she will be disappointed
    (C) because she will have a disappointment
    (D) on account of she will be disappointed
    (E) because she shall be disappointed

40. My younger brother insists <u>that he is as tall as me.</u>

    (A) that he is as tall as me
    (B) that he is so tall as me
    (C) that he is tall as me
    (D) that he is as tall as I
    (E) he is as tall as me

Directions: The sentences below contain errors in grammar, usage, word choice, and idiom. Parts of each sentence are underlined and lettered. Decide which underlined part contains the error and mark its letter on your answer sheet. If the sentence is correct as it stands, mark (E) on your answer sheet. No sentence contains more than one error.

41. The <u>boy,</u> <u>as well as</u> his mother, <u>desperately</u>
       A   B   C
    <u>need</u> help. <u>No error.</u>
     D   E

42. <u>While</u> the play was <u>in progress,</u> several mem-
     A   B
    bers of the audience <u>walk</u> out and demanded
                 C
    their money <u>back.</u> <u>No error.</u>
           D   E

43. <u>Everyone</u> of the tenants must <u>refuse</u> to pay <u>his</u>
     A   B   C
    <u>or her</u> rent until the repairs are completed and
    heat <u>is restored.</u> <u>No error.</u>
         D   E

44. In Shanghai we will <u>be sure to</u> visit the French
                  A
    sector, where rich families <u>use</u> <u>to reside</u> in el-
                  B   C
    egant <u>villas.</u> <u>No error.</u>
       D   E

45. The High Gothic cathedrals of France, <u>erected</u>
                            A
    in the thirteenth century <u>at enormous cost,</u> <u>may</u>
                       B   C

be <u>regarded</u> as monuments to the religious fer-

$\overline{\hspace{1.5em}}$ D

vor of the age. <u>No error</u>.

     E

46. The speaker <u>issued</u> a triple challenge: to stu-

    A

dents to work hard, to parents to encourage <u>their</u>

             B

<u>children's</u> studies, and to educators <u>in</u> empha-

C   D

sizing basic skills. <u>No error</u>.

       E

47. Astronomers recently <u>identifying</u> a giant spiral

       A

galaxy in the constellation Camelopardus, which

they say is the largest and <u>most massive</u> <u>so far</u>

        B   C

<u>sighted</u> in the universe. <u>No error</u>.

D   E

48. Those <u>kind</u> of musical <u>compositions</u> are so <u>dis-</u>

   A   B   C

sonant that I find <u>it</u> difficult to listen to them.

       D

<u>No error</u>.

E

49. <u>Having lived</u> for many years <u>under</u> the tyranny

A   B

of the emperor Domitian, the Roman historian

Tacitus <u>detested</u> the imperial form of govern-

   C

ment and <u>would have liked</u> to have seen a return

      D

to the republican form. <u>No error</u>.

       E

50. Rescue workers reported that the flood, <u>which</u>

            A

<u>had swept</u> through the village about dawn, left

B

three people <u>drownded</u> and <u>forty-one</u> families

    C   D

homeless. <u>No error</u>.

   E

STOP

END OF SECTION III. IF YOU HAVE ANY TIME LEFT, GO OVER YOUR WORK IN THIS SECTION ONLY. DO NOT WORK IN ANY OTHER SECTION OF THE TEST.

SECTION IV: MATHEMATICAL ABILITIES

35 Questions
Time—30 Minutes

Directions: The following problems are to be solved using any available space on the page for scratchwork. When a problem has been worked out, mark your answer on the answer sheet.

The following information should be helpful in determining the correct answers for some of the problems:

Circle of radius r: Area = πr^2; Circumference = $2\pi r$. The number of degrees of an arc in a circle is 360. The measure of degrees of a straight angle is 180.

Definitions of symbols:

∥ is parallel to   > is greater than
≦ is less than or equal to   < is less than
≧ is greater than or equal to   ⊥ is perpendicular to
∠ angle   △ triangle

Triangle: The sum of the measures in degrees of the angles is 180. The angle BDC is a right angle; therefore,

(1) the area of triangle ABC = $\dfrac{AC \times BD}{2}$

(2) $AB^2 = AD^2 + DB^2$

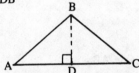

Note: The figures accompanying the problems are drawn as accurately as possible unless otherwise stated in specific problems. Again, unless otherwise stated, all figures lie in the same plane. All numbers used in these problems are real numbers.

1. The tiles in the floor of a bathroom are $^{15}/_{16}$ inch squares. The cement between the tiles is $^1/_{16}$ inch. There are 3,240 individual tiles in this floor. The area of the floor is

   (A) 225 sq. yds.
   (B) 2.5 sq. yds.
   (C) 250 sq. ft.
   (D) 22.5 sq. yds.
   (E) 225 sq. ft.

2. Of the following, the one that is *not* equivalent to 376 is

   (A) $(3 \times 100) + (6 \times 10) + 16$
   (B) $(2 \times 100) + (17 \times 10) + 6$
   (C) $(3 \times 100) + (7 \times 10) + 6$
   (D) $(2 \times 100) + (16 \times 10) + 6$
   (E) $(2 \times 100) + (7 \times 10) + 106$

3. A man bought a TV set that was listed at $160. He was given successive discounts of 20% and 10%. The price he paid was

   (A) $112.00
   (B) $115.20
   (C) $119.60
   (D) $129.60
   (E) $118.20

4. The total length of fencing needed to enclose a rectangular area 46 feet by 34 feet is

   (A) 26 yards 1 foot
   (B) 26⅔ yards
   (C) 52 yards 2 feet
   (D) 53⅓ yards
   (E) 37⅔ yards

5. A clerk's income for a year is $15,000. He pays 15% of this in federal taxes and 10% of the remainder for state taxes. How much is left?

   (A) $12,750
   (B) $9,750
   (C) $14,125
   (D) $13,500
   (E) $11,475

6. $(x^a)^b =$

   (A) $x \cdot a \cdot b$
   (B) x^{a+b}
   (C) x^{ab}
   (D) y^{ax}
   (E) b^{xa}

7. A is 300 miles from B. The path of all points equidistant from A and B can best be described as

   (A) a line ∥ to AB and 150 miles north of AB
   (B) a transverse segment cutting through AB at a 45° angle

Directions: For the following items compare two quantities, one in Column A and one in Column B, and determine whether:
(A) the quantity is greater in Column A
(B) the quantity is greater in Column B
(C) both quantities are equal
(D) no comparison can be made with the information given

Notes: (1) Information concerning one or both of the compared quantities will be centered between the two columns for some of the items.
(2) Symbols that appear in both columns represent the same thing in Column A as in Column B.
(3) Letters such as x, n, and k are symbols for real numbers.
(4) Do not mark choice (E), as there are only four choices.

COLUMN A	COLUMN B

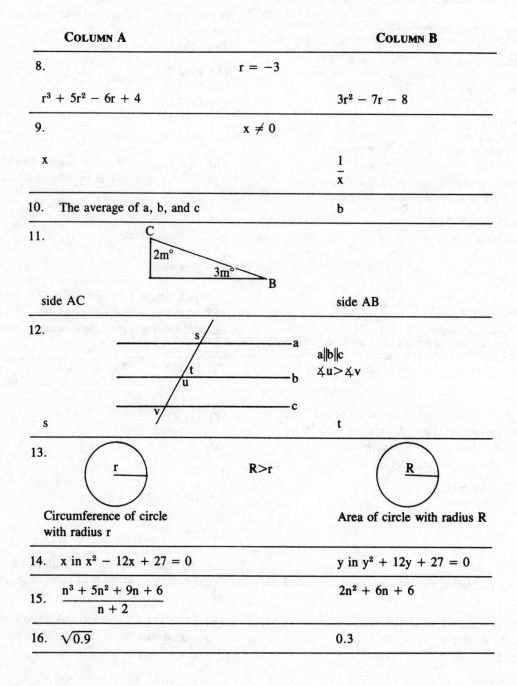

8. $r = -3$

$r^3 + 5r^2 - 6r + 4$ | $3r^2 - 7r - 8$

9. $x \neq 0$

x | $\dfrac{1}{x}$

10. The average of a, b, and c | b

11.

side AC | side AB

12.

$a\|b\|c$
$\angle u > \angle v$

s | t

13. $R > r$

Circumference of circle with radius r | Area of circle with radius R

14. x in $x^2 - 12x + 27 = 0$ | y in $y^2 + 12y + 27 = 0$

15. $\dfrac{n^3 + 5n^2 + 9n + 6}{n + 2}$ | $2n^2 + 6n + 6$

16. $\sqrt{0.9}$ | 0.3

Column A		**Column B**
17.	s>t	
s²		t²

Questions 26–28 refer to the figure below.

18.

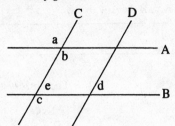

C ∥ D
A ∥ B

a + b	a = 100°	b + d
19. 180°		b + c
20. d		180° − a
21.	(½)x − (½)a = 4	
x		a
22. 6% of 200		7% of 300

23.

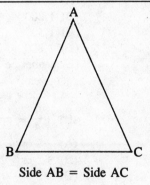

Side AB = Side AC

∡A		∡B

24.

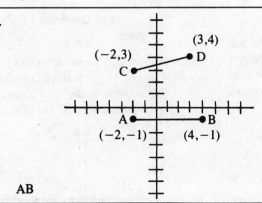

AB		CD

COLUMN A	COLUMN B

25.

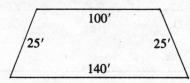

$\angle$ m $80° - \angle$ n

26. $(\frac{1}{4}) * 2$ $A * B = A/4 + 2B$ $5 * (\frac{1}{2})$

27. $\sqrt[3]{8x^3y^6}$ $2xy^3$

Directions: Solve each of the remaining problems in this section using any available space for scratchwork.

28. A merchant sold two radios for $120 each. One was sold at a loss of 25% of the cost, and the other was sold at a gain of 25% of the cost. On both transactions combined, the merchant lost

   (A) $64.00
   (B) $36.00
   (C) $16.00
   (D) $30.00
   (E) $0.00

29. The number missing in the series 2, 6, 12, 20, ?, 42, 56, 72 is

   (A) 38
   (B) 40
   (C) 36
   (D) 24
   (E) 30

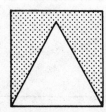

30. The square and the equilateral triangle in the above drawing both have a side of 6. If the triangle is placed inside the square with one side of the triangle directly on one side of the square, what is the area of the shaded region?

   (A) $36 - 6\sqrt{3}$
   (B) $36 + 6\sqrt{3}$
   (C) $36 + 9\sqrt{3}$
   (D) $36 - 9\sqrt{3}$
   (E) $36 - 18\sqrt{3}$

31. The closest approximation to the value $\sqrt{2/5}$ is

   (A) .6
   (B) $\frac{1}{5}$
   (C) .16
   (D) .4
   (E) .28

32. One end of a dam has the shape of a trapezoid with the dimensions indicated. What is the dam's area in square feet?

   (A) 1,000
   (B) 1,200
   (C) 1,500
   (D) 1,800
   (E) cannot be determined from the information given

33. If $1 + \frac{1}{t} = \frac{t+1}{t}$, what does t equal?

   (A) +2 only
   (B) +2 or −2 only
   (C) +2 or −1 only
   (D) −2 or +1 only
   (E) cannot be determined from the information given

34. Point A is 3 inches from line b as shown in the diagram. In the plane that contains point A and line b, what is the total number of points that are 6 inches from A and also 1 inch from b?

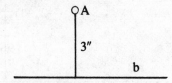

(A) 0
(B) 1
(C) 2
(D) 3
(E) 4

35. If R and S are integers both divisible by 5, then which of the following is *not necessarily* true?

(A) R − S is divisible by 5
(B) RS is divisible by 25
(C) R + S is divisible by 5
(D) $R^2 + S^2$ is divisible by 5
(E) R + S is divisible by 10

STOP

END OF SECTION IV. IF YOU HAVE ANY TIME LEFT, GO OVER YOUR WORK IN THIS SECTION ONLY. DO NOT WORK IN ANY OTHER SECTION OF THE TEST.

SECTION V: VERBAL ABILITIES

40 Questions
Time—30 Minutes

Directions: Each of the following items contains a word in capital letters, followed by five words or phrases. Select the word or phrase most nearly *opposite* in meaning to the capitalized word.

1. OBSTINATE :

   (A) grateful
   (B) intelligent
   (C) vengeful
   (D) jealous
   (E) cooperative

2. RANCOR :

   (A) dignity
   (B) affection
   (C) odor
   (D) spite
   (E) suspicion

3. CAPRICIOUS :

   (A) active
   (B) stable
   (C) opposed
   (D) sheeplike
   (E) slippery

4. CRYPTIC :

   (A) appealing
   (B) arched
   (C) deathly
   (D) revealing
   (E) intricate

5. PERSEVERANCE :

   (A) disclosure
   (B) tranquility
   (C) reasonableness
   (D) cessation
   (E) moderation

6. SATURATED :

   (A) hidden
   (B) foreign
   (C) barren
   (D) bland
   (E) explicit

7. ATROCIOUS :

   (A) pliable
   (B) excellent
   (C) playful
   (D) normal
   (E) inappropriate

8. INTELLIGIBLE :

   (A) careful
   (B) unclear
   (C) faulty
   (D) stubborn
   (E) unteachable

9. UPROOT :

   (A) overtake
   (B) express
   (C) weigh
   (D) obey
   (E) insert

10. ANIMOSITY :

   (A) reliability
   (B) avidity
   (C) thoughtfulness
   (D) anxiety
   (E) friendliness

Directions: Each of the following sentences contains one or two blank spaces to be filled in by one of the five choices listed below each sentence. Select the word or words that *best* complete the meaning of the sentence.

11. The council of ministers _____ the spread of _____ violence.

   (A) lamented—sensible
   (B) denounced—senile
   (C) lauded—random

128

(D) deplored—needless

(E) dismissed—senseless

12. Her _____ smile _____ all those who saw it.

   (A) devastating—blinded
   (B) penultimate—inured
   (C) radiant—obliged
   (D) sunny—tanned
   (E) bright—dazzled

13. Although he was known as a _____ old miser, his _____ gifts to charity were always anonymous.

   (A) grasping—tasteless
   (B) spendthrift—gracious
   (C) gregarious—selfish
   (D) penurious—generous
   (E) stingy—mangy

14. With one _____ motion, Brian disarmed his assailant and gained his freedom.

   (A) maladroit
   (B) deft
   (C) ponderous
   (D) graceful
   (E) brusque

15. *Vanities* started as a _____ magazine, appearing the first and third week of each month.

   (A) biennial
   (B) bimonthly
   (C) semimonthly
   (D) periodical
   (E) quarterly

Directions: Each of the following items contains a pair of words in capital letters, followed by five pairs of words. Choose the pair that *best* expresses a relationship similar to the one expressed by the capitalized pair.

16. TEACHER : INSTRUCTION ::

   (A) lawyer : legal
   (B) army : fights
   (C) doctor : heals
   (D) watchman : protection
   (E) student : learn

17. HOSTESS : RESTAURANT ::

   (A) receptionist : office

(B) bartender : tavern

(C) porter : railroad

(D) friendly : delicious

(E) cowboy : range

18. SKATE : RINK ::

   (A) contest : arena
   (B) bowling : alley
   (C) repose : bed
   (D) sports : stadium
   (E) ice : circle

19. SAPLING : TREE ::

   (A) weed : plant
   (B) grass : wheat
   (C) puppy : dog
   (D) seed : vegetable
   (E) acorn : oak

20. FRET : RELAX ::

   (A) worry : problems
   (B) sob : cry
   (C) fight : submit
   (D) sing : laugh
   (E) guitar : play

21. STUTTER : TALK ::

   (A) worry : problems
   (B) stumble : walk
   (C) walk : run
   (D) hear : understand
   (E) mistake : perfect

22. DESTROY : DEMOLISH ::

   (A) cry : wail
   (B) break : mar
   (C) slack : looseness
   (D) strict : lax
   (E) plan : action

23. FUNNEL : LIQUID ::

   (A) hose : water
   (B) speaker : sound
   (C) window : air
   (D) vent : smoke
   (E) chimney : fumes

24. QUALITY : QUANTITY ::

    (A) good : number
    (B) characteristic : volume
    (C) success : mass
    (D) govern : elect
    (E) optimist : pessimist

25. CONDUCTOR : ORCHESTRA ::

    (A) captain : sports
    (B) employer : employee
    (C) coach : team
    (D) director : playing
    (E) teacher : music

Directions: Each of the following reading passages is followed by a set of questions. Read each passage and answer the accompanying questions, basing your answers on what is *stated* or *implied* in the passage.

Hong Kong's size and association with Britain, and its position in relation to its neighbors in the Pacific, particularly China, determine the course of conduct it has to pursue. Hong Kong is no more than a molecule in the great substance of China. It was part of the large province of Kwangtung, which came under Chinese sovereignty about 200 B.C., in the period of the Han Dynasty. In size, China exceeds 3¾ million square miles, and it has a population estimated to be greater than 700 million. Its very immensity has contributed to its survival over a great period of time. Without probing into the origins of its remarkable civilization, we can mark that it has a continuous history of more than 4,000 years. And, through the centuries, it has always been able to defend itself in depth, trading space for time.

In this setting Hong Kong is minute. Its area is a mere 398 square miles, about one two-hundredth part of the province of which it was previously part, Kwangtung. Fortunately, however, we cannot dispose of Hong Kong as simply as this. There are components in its complex and unique existence which affect its character and, out of all physical proportion, increase its significance.

Amongst these, the most potent are its people, their impressive achievements in partnership with British administration and enterprise, and the rule of law which protects personal freedom in the British tradition.

What is Hong Kong, and what is it trying to do? In 1841 Britain acquired outright, by treaty, the Island of Hong Kong, to use as a base for trade with China, and, in 1860, the Kowloon Peninsula, lying immediately to the north, to complete the perimeter of the superb harbour, which has determined Hong Kong's history and character. In 1898 Britain leased for 99 years a hinterland on the mainland of China to a depth of less than 25 miles, much of it very hilly. Hong Kong prospered as a center of trade with China, expanding steadily until it fell to the Japanese in 1941. Although the rigors of a severe occupation set everything back, the Liberation in 1945 was the herald of an immediate and spectacular recovery in trade. People poured into the Colony, and this flow became a flood during 1949-50, when the Chinese National Government met defeat at the hands of the Communists. Three-quarters of a million people entered the Colony at that stage, bringing the total population to 2⅓ millions. Today the population is more than 3¾ millions.

Very soon two things affected commercial expansion. First, the Chinese Government restricted Hong Kong's exports to China, because she feared unsettled internal conditions, mounting inflation and a weakness in her exchange position. Secondly, during the Korean War, the United Nations imposed an embargo on imports into China, the main source of Hong Kong's livelihood. This was a crisis for Hong Kong; its China trade went overnight, and, by this time, it had over one million refugees on its hands. But something dramatic happened. Simply stated, it was this: Hong Kong switched from trading to manufacture. It did it so quickly that few people, even in Hong Kong, were aware at the time of what exactly was happening, and the rest of the world was not quickly convinced of Hong Kong's transformation into a center of manufactures. Its limited industry began to expand rapidly and, although more slowly, to diversify, and it owed not a little to the immigrants from Shanghai, who brought their capital, their experience and expertise with them. Today Hong Kong must be unique amongst so-called developing countries in the dependence of its economy on industrialization. No less than 40 per cent of the labor force is engaged in the manufacturing industries; and of the products from these Hong Kong exports 90 per cent, and it does this despite the fact that its industry is exposed to the full competition of the industrially mature nations. The variety of its goods now ranges widely from the products of shipbuilding and shipbreaking, through textiles and plastics, to air-conditioners, transistor radios and cameras.

More than 70 per cent of its exports are either manufactured or partly manufactured in Hong Kong, and the value of its domestic exports in 1964 was about 750 million dollars. In recent years these figures have been increasing at about 15 per cent a year. America is the largest market, taking 25 per cent of the value of Hong Kong's exports: then follows the United Kingdom, Malaysia, West Germany, Japan, Canada and Australia; but all countries come within the scope of its marketing.

26. The article gives the impression that

    (A) English rule constituted an important factor in the Hong Kong economy
    (B) refugees from China were a liability to the financial status of Hong Kong
    (C) Hong Kong has taken a developmental course comparable to that of the new African nations
    (D) British forces used their military might imperialistically to acquire Hong Kong
    (E) there is a serious dearth of skilled workers in Hong Kong

27. The economic stability of Hong Kong is mostly attributable to

    (A) its shipbuilding activity
    (B) businessmen and workers from Shanghai who settled in Hong Kong
    (C) its political separation from China
    (D) its exports to China
    (E) a change in the area of business concentration

28. Hong Kong's commerce was adversely affected by

    (A) the Han Dynasty
    (B) Japanese occupation
    (C) British administration
    (D) the defeat of the Chinese National Government
    (E) the conversion from manufacturing to trading

29. According to the passage the population of China exceeds that of Hong Kong by approximately

    (A) 300 million
    (B) 600 million
    (C) 700 million
    (D) 900 million
    (E) 1 billion

30. The author states or implies that

    (A) the United States imports more goods from Hong Kong than all the other nations combined
    (B) about three quarters of its exports are made exclusively in Hong Kong
    (C) Malaysia, Canada, and West Germany provide excellent markets for Hong Kong goods
    (D) approximately one half of the Hong Kong workers are involved with manufacturing
    (E) the United Nations has consistently cooperated to improve the economy of Hong Kong

Contemporary astronomy is ordinarily at least as much of an observational as a theoretical science. Sooner or later on the basis of observation and analysis, what astronomers detect finds its way into theory, or the theory is modified to accept it.

Neutrino astronomy doesn't fit this pattern. Its highly developed body of theory grew for 30 years without any possibility of verification. And despite the construction, finally, of a string of elaborate observatories, some buried in the earth from southern India to Utah to South Africa, the last five years as well have produced not a single, validated observation of an extraterrestrial neutrino.

It is a testament to the persistence of the neutrino astronomers and to the strength of their theoretical base that their intensive search for these ghost particles still goes on.

The neutrino is a particle with a vanishingly small mass and no charge. Having no charge, it does not interact with the fields around which most particle detection experiments are built; it can be detected only inferentially, by identification of the debris left following its rare interaction with matter.

Even such indirect observations need elaborate and highly sensitive equipment which didn't begin to go into place until about five years ago. But the goal is worth the effort: once detected, extraterrestrial neutrinos will provide solid, firsthand information on the sources and conditions that spawned them.

Scientists are sure of this because of the sophistication of experiments on neutrino reactions in particle accelerators and other earth-bound apparatus. These experiments have been refined rigorously over the years, and neutrino theory based on them is an integral part of modern physics.

The existence of neutrinos was first postulated in

the early 1930s, in order to explain a form of radio-active decay in which a beta particle—an electron—is emitted. Certain quantities that physicists insist should be the same after an interaction as before—momentum, energy, and angular momentum—could only be conserved if another particle of zero charge and negligible mass were emitted.

31. This article was written for the purpose of

    (A) detailing the work of astronomers
    (B) reviewing the search for neutrinos
    (C) discussing the theory of astronomy
    (D) describing the dangers of neutrinos
    (E) explaining the uses of neutrinos

32. The neutrino was first discovered by scientists through

    (A) actual observation
    (B) the use of telescopes
    (C) the use of a microscope
    (D) guessing
    (E) the use of a computer

33. In size the neutrino is

    (A) too small to be observed
    (B) slightly larger than a neutron
    (C) slightly larger than a proton
    (D) the smallest thing ever observed
    (E) the same size as the smallest atom

34. The author feels that neutrino theory

    (A) was developed to aid astronomers in space observation with their telescopes
    (B) will never be proven
    (C) has become a proven fact
    (D) is now an accepted part of scientific knowledge
    (E) was based entirely on indirect observation

35. The neutrino theory developed as a result of which of the following laws?

    (A) magnetism
    (B) conservation
    (C) inertia
    (D) motion
    (E) observation

The modern belief that man's institutions can accomplish just about anything he wants, when he wants it, leads to certain characteristic contemporary phenomena.

One is the bitterness and anger toward our institutions that well up when high hopes turn sour. No observer of the modern scene has failed to note the prevalent cynicism concerning all leaders, all officials, all social institutions. That cynicism is continually fed and renewed by the rage of people who expected too much in the first place and got too little in the end.

The aspirations are healthy. But soaring hope followed by rude disappointment is a formula for trouble. Leaders arise whose whole stock in trade is to exploit first the aspirations and then the disappointment. They profit on both the ups and downs of the market.

All of this leaves us with some crucial and puzzling questions of public policy. How can we make sluggish institutions more responsive to human need and the requirements of change? How can we mobilize the resources to meet the grave crises ahead?

How can we preserve our aspirations (without which no social betterment is possible) and at the same time develop the toughness of mind and spirit to face the fact that there are no easy victories?

How can we make people understand that if they expect all good things instantly, they will destroy everything? How do we tell them that they must keep unrelenting pressure on their social institutions to accomplish beneficial change but must not, in a fit of rage, destroy those institutions? How can we caution them against exploitative leaders, leaders lustful for power or for the spotlight, leaders caught in their own vanity or emotional instability, leaders selling extremist ideologies?

How can we dimish the resort to violence? Violence cannot build a better society. No society can live in constant and destructive tumult. Either we will have a civil order in which discipline is internalized in the breast of each free and responsible citizen, or sooner or later we will have repressive measures designed to reestablish order. The anarchist plays into the hands of the authoritarian. Those of us who find authoritarianism repugnant have a duty to speak out against all who destroy civil order. The time has come when the full weight of community opinion should be felt by those who break the peace or coerce through mob action.

Dissent is an element of dynamism in our system. It is good that men should expect much of their institutions, good that their aspirations for improvement of this society should be ardent.

But those elements of dynamism must have their stabilizing counterparts. One is a tough-minded recognition that the fight for a better world is a long one, a recognition that retains high hopes but immunizes against childish collapse or destructive rage in the face of disappointment. The other is an unswerving commitment to keep the public peace.

And we need something else. An increasing number of bright and able people must become involved in the development of public policy. Ours is a difficult and exhilarating form of government—not for the faint of heart, not for the tidy-minded, and in these days of complexity not for the stupid. We need men and women who can bring to government the highest order of intellect, social motivations sturdy enough to pursue good purposes despite setbacks, and a resilience of spirit equal to the frustrations of public life.

36. The basic purpose of this selection is to

(A) offer solutions
(B) criticize our institutions
(C) plead for moderation
(D) lessen expectations
(E) solve our problems

37. It can be inferred that high aspirations

(A) result in a dynamic society
(B) are a waste of time

(C) are dangerous to society
(D) take time to be fulfilled
(E) are the result of being misled

38. The author suggests that one of the greatest contributions to strife and violence at present is

(A) history
(B) dynamism
(C) politicians
(D) society
(E) institutions

39. Regarding the qualities desired in a public official, all of the following are mentioned *except*

(A) motivation
(B) intelligence
(C) patience
(D) education
(E) honesty

40. It is the feeling of the author that those who practice social disorder

(A) have high aspirations
(B) lust for power
(C) are victims of our institutions
(D) help the oppressors
(E) are our true leaders

STOP

END OF SECTION V. IF YOU HAVE ANY TIME LEFT, GO OVER YOUR WORK IN THIS SECTION ONLY. DO NOT WORK IN ANY OTHER SECTION OF THE TEST.

ANSWER KEY

Section I

1. D	10. A	19. D	28. B	37. C
2. C	11. D	20. C	29. D	38. D
3. D	12. A	21. C	30. A	39. A
4. D	13. E	22. E	31. B	40. C
5. B	14. A	23. D	32. E	41. A
6. D	15. A	24. C	33. A	42. D
7. D	16. B	25. A	34. D	43. C
8. D	17. A	26. B	35. E	44. A
9. C	18. B	27. A	36. B	45. E

Section II

1. A	6. C	11. A	16. E	21. E
2. B	7. C	12. B	17. C	22. B
3. C	8. E	13. B	18. E	23. B
4. C	9. D	14. E	19. E	24. A
5. B	10. C	15. E	20. B	25. D

Section III

1. A	11. D	21. D	31. E	41. D
2. C	12. A	22. D	32. C	42. C
3. B	13. C	23. E	33. B	43. A
4. C	14. D	24. C	34. A	44. B
5. A	15. C	25. E	35. D	45. E
6. C	16. C	26. D	36. C	46. D
7. E	17. E	27. D	37. E	47. A
8. D	18. A	28. E	38. C	48. A
9. B	19. B	29. B	39. B	49. E
10. E	20. C	30. A	40. D	50. C

Section IV

1. B	8. C	15. B	22. B	29. E
2. D	9. D	16. A	23. D	30. D
3. B	10. D	17. D	24. A	31. A
4. D	11. A	18. A	25. D	32. D
5. E	12. A	19. B	26. A	33. E
6. C	13. D	20. C	27. D	34. E
7. D	14. A	21. A	28. C	35. E

Section V

1. E	9. E	17. A	25. C	33. A
2. B	10. E	18. C	26. A	34. D
3. B	11. D	19. C	27. E	35. B
4. D	12. E	20. C	28. B	36. C
5. D	13. D	21. B	29. C	37. D
6. C	14. B	22. A	30. C	38. C
7. B	15. C	23. E	31. B	39. D
8. B	16. D	24. B	32. D	40. D

EXPLANATORY ANSWERS

Section I

1. **(D)** To *minimize* is to "reduce to a minimum," whereas to *expand* is to "increase or enlarge."

2. **(C)** What is *monotonous* is "tediously uniform" and hence boring. What is *exciting* is "rousing" and hence not boring.

3. **(D)** To *innovate* is to "produce something new," whereas to *copy* is merely to "reproduce something already given."

4. **(D)** To be *omnipotent* is to be "all-powerful," whereas to be *weak* is to be "lacking in power."

5. **(B)** An *amateur* "engages in a pursuit as a pastime," whereas a *professional* "engages in a pursuit as a profession."

6. **(D)** A *downfall* is "a sudden fall from a high position or rank," whereas a *success* is an "attainment of some rank, position, or goal."

7. **(D)** To *eulogize* is to "speak in high praise of something," whereas to *berate* is to "condemn something."

8. **(D)** Something *turgid* is in "a state of enlargement or expansion," whereas something *deflated* is "reduced in size."

9. **(C)** To *expunge* is to "strike or mark out something," whereas to *perpetuate* is to "cause something to last indefinitely."

10. **(A)** To suffer *ignominy* is to suffer "personal humiliation and disgrace," whereas to gain *fame* is to gain "public recognition."

11. **(D)** What is *relevant* has a "bearing upon and is appropriate to the subject under discussion" and hence is the opposite of *inappropriate*.

12. **(A)** To *disparage* is to "express a low estimation of something," whereas to *applaud* is to "express a high estimation of something."

13. **(E)** What is *opulent* is "wealthy or abundant," while what is *impoverished* is "poor or deprived of resources."

14. **(A)** To *propitiate* is to "regain the goodwill of someone"; to *anger* means to "enrage."

15. **(A)** Someone who is *devious* is "not straightforward," whereas someone who is *candid* is "straightforward."

16. **(B)** Acting together, those involved would be *responsible* for an *element*.

17. **(A)** Unwise *neglect* during someone's education could result in *ignorance*.

18. **(B)** Communist countries deny the *rhetoric*—not the economy or decline—of capitalist ones and have been *without*—not *negotiating* or *admitting*—"success of suppressing it."

19. **(D)** A policeman might be *forgetful* of his duties and *release* a prisoner.

20. **(C)** To insure a stronger market network, a profit-minded top-level management might decide to *improve* operations in "*unattended* (or neglected) market areas."

21. **(C)** The author does not like the art of the period following the French Revolution, so answers (B), (D), and (E), suggestive of development, improvement, or appeal, are wrong responses. As there is no evidence to support choice (A), and answer (C) is appropriately negative, answer (C) is the correct response.

22. **(E)** Only answer (E)—religion—was not specifically mentioned as affecting art in the 1870s. This, then, is the correct response. The author felt that photography (A) produced total accuracy, that the war (B) brought about a loss of ability to idealize, and that objectivism (C) no longer existed. His harshest comments were directed toward the trend of naturalism (D) in art.

23. **(D)** Although answer (B) seems to be the ap-

propriate response, it is not correct. The naturalism that the author so vehemently attacks is repulsive to him because it is "devoid of poetry" and needs to be revitalized with elegance. It is not so much the naturalism he dislikes as it is the apparent lack of elegance. Choice (D) is therefore the best answer here.

24. **(C)** The author likes least the portraits of Francis Peters, wherein he sees naturalism as an end in itself. (C) is the correct answer. He is not pleased with Green (A) but writes less harshly of him. He writes positively of Singer (B), Bolati (D), and Walter (E); however, these are poor responses to the question.

25. **(A)** The author writes of the war, naturalism, and photography as having disastrous effects on the art of the mid-1800s. His main purpose, then, is to discuss the reasons for these phenomena, and answer (A) is the appropriate choice. Answers (B) and (C), although discussed quite fully, do not express the thrust of the entire passage. (D) and (E) cannot be supported from the information given.

26. **(B)** Answer (A) is a wrong choice. Reference is made only to the lower cost of carrying out a CB program. It cannot be concluded that its control would be less costly. Choices (C) and (E) are also incorrect, as smaller nations *are* involved in such systems. Answer (D) appears to be a sensible response, but the article also moots the importance of controlling nuclear warfare programs. (B) is the best response. Because of the growing involvement of many smaller nations and the relatively lower cost of CB programs, controls may not be possible or desirable.

27. **(A)** Among the choices only (A) is not mentioned as a cause for the continued development of CB weapons. Answer (A) is the correct choice.

28. **(B)** The British journalist does not imply any of the statements suggested in answers (A), (C), (D), or (E). He does suggest, however, development and continued research among the major powers as a fear tactic. Choice (B) is the correct answer.

29. **(D)** "The large and expensive programs in the United States and the Soviet Union are attributed to each other's 'large and expensive programs.'" Therefore, the U.S. feels justified in having such a program because Russia has one. (D) is the correct choice. There is not enough information given to support answers (A), (B), or (E). Answer (C) is a true statement, but it is not the main reason for employing CB programs.

30. **(A)** Answer (A) best reflects the main purpose of the article and is the correct response to the question. Answers (B) and (C) are mentioned in the article but do not constitute the main purpose for writing it. There is little in the article to indicate (D) or (E) as the correct response.

31. **(B)** The faith of the members of this parish is not *incomparable, unusual, unregimented*, or *unlikely*, but it is *unwavering*.

32. **(E)** *Unsteady* is similar to *changing*.

33. **(A)** Congestion and pollution make cities *unlivable*, not necessarily *fatal, cosmopolitan, delineated*, or *empty*.

34. **(D)** *Ease* might mitigate the experience of taking the examination, but it might not compensate for earlier heavy pressure.

35. **(E)** A client does not *contest, dismiss, fulfill*, or *recommend* his own case to his lawyer. (E) is the answer.

36. **(B)** An *awl* is used to *puncture*, and a *cleaver* is used to *cut*.

37. **(C)** A *lush* area cannot be *barren*, and a *jungle* cannot be a *desert*.

38. **(D)** If something is *gnarled*, it will necessarily be *curved*; if something is *inflexible*, it will necessarily be *stiff*.

39. **(A)** If something is *spinning*, it is *revolving*; if something is *traveling*, it is *moving*.

40. **(C)** *Air* that *stagnates* loses its original freshness. *Wood* that *rots* deteriorates from its original condition.

41. **(A)** The relationship is one of synonyms. The only pair of synonyms among the answer choices is (A).

42. **(D)** A *scientist* works in a *laboratory* and a *teacher* works in a *classroom*.

43. **(C)** The *program* is the set of directions that the *computer* follows. The *recipe* is the set of directions that a *cook* follows. Although one might argue that there are weaknesses in this analogy, the student is reminded that the directions say to pick the best answer, not a flawless answer.

44. **(A)** *Jocular* is the opposite of *solemn*; *latent* is the opposite of *perceptible*.

45. **(E)** A *stockholder* receives *dividends* and a *songwriter* receives *royalties*.

Section II

1. **(A)**

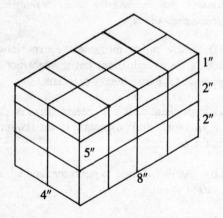

The 2-inch ice cube will fit only in the 8-inch by 4-inch by 4-inch part of the compartment. The upper inch cannot be used.

Hence, $\dfrac{8 \times 4 \times 4}{2 \times 2 \times 2} = 16$ cubes

2. **(B)** Draw OP. Then in right triangle OPS,
$OP^2 = PS^2 + OS^2 = 6^2 + 8^2 = 10^2$
$OP = 10$
Then $\overarc{QR} = \frac{1}{4} \cdot 2\pi r = \frac{1}{4} \cdot 2\pi \cdot 10 = 5\pi$

3. **(C)**

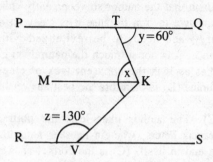

Through point K, draw KM parallel to PQ and RS. Then
$\angle x = \angle MKV + \angle MKT$
$\angle MKV = \angle KVS = 180 - 130 = 50°$
$\angle MKT = \angle QTK = 60°$
Then $\angle x = 60° + 50° = 110°$

4. **(C)** This is easily solved by plugging in the numbers:
$(4 - 1) \times (5 - 2) \times (6 - 3) = 3 \times 3 \times 3 = 27.$

5. **(B)** $\angle TSP = 60°$
Since $PSR = 90°$, $\angle TSR = 90 - 60 = 30°$
Since $TS = PS = SR$, $\angle RTS = \angle TRS$
Thus, $\angle TRS = \frac{1}{2} (180° - 30°) = \frac{1}{2} (150°) = 75°$

6. **(C)** Setting up a ratio, 88 ft./sec.:60 mi./hr. as 1100 ft./sec.:x mi./hr. $88x = (1100)(60)$, so $x = 750$ mi./hr.

7. **(C)** If 2n is an even number, $2n + 1$ is odd. $2n + 2n + 1 = 4n + 1$, which is always odd.

8. **(E)** Let x be the second angle. The first angle is 3x, the third angle is $x + 20$. The angles of a triangle must equal 180°, so $3x + x + (x + 20) = 180$, $5x = 160$, $x = 32$.

9. **(D)** Setting up a ratio, ¼ in.:12 in. as 3⅜ in.:x in. $(\frac{1}{4})x = (12)(3\frac{3}{8})$, $x = 162$ in. (1 ft./12 in.) = 13½ ft.

10. **(C)** When we are given the diagonal of a square, we can find the length of the side by dividing the diagonal by two and multiplying by $\sqrt{2}$.

11. **(A)** $14 + 17 = 31$. Therefore, there are 4

students who must be enrolled in all three courses. $^4/_{27}$ is slightly larger than $^4/_{28}$. The answer must be slightly larger than $^1/_7$, which is $14^2/_7\%$.

12. **(B)** The volume of the container is the area of the circle at one end times the height. The area of the circle is $A = \pi 7^2 \approx 154$ sq. in. The volume is $154 \times 6 = 924$ cu. in. The capacity of the tank is 924 cu. in. $\div$ 231 cu. in./gal. = 4 gallons.

13. **(B)** Let the time the train is scheduled to arrive be t. At 40 mi./hr. the train arrives in $t + ^{10}/_{60} = t + ^1/_6$ hours. At 30 mi./hr. the train takes $t + ^{16}/_{60} = t + ^4/_{15}$ hours. The distance is the speed times the time. $d = 40$ mi./hr. $\times$ ($t + ^1/_6$) hr. = 30 mi./hr. $\times$ ($t + ^4/_{15}$). Solving one finds $40(t + ^1/_6) = 30(t + ^4/_{15}) = > 40t + ^{40}/_6 = 30t + 8 = > t = ^8/_{60}$ hr. The distance between towns is $d = (40$ mi./hr.) $(^8/_{60} + ^{10}/_{60})$ hr. $= 40 \times ^{18}/_{60} = 12$ miles.

14. **(E)** Since it takes Paul 2 hours to paint 1 fence, he paints ½ of the fence in one hour. Fred paints ⅓ of the fence per hour. Together their speed is $½ + ⅓ = ^5/_6$ fence/hr. The time to paint this fence together is 1 fence $\div$ $^5/_6$ fence/hr. = 1.2 hours.

15. **(E)** The time it takes the driver to arrive at her destination is 60 miles $\div$ 40 miles per hour = 1½ hours. The time it takes to return is 60 miles $\div$ 30 miles per hour = 2 hours, making the total time for this 120 mile trip 1½ + 2 = 3½ hours. The average speed for the entire trip is 120 miles $\div$ 3½ hours = $34^2/_7$ miles per hour.

16. **(E)** If there are 28.35 grams per ounce, then 28.35 grams per ounce $\div$ 1000 grams per kilogram = .02835 kilograms per ounce. Since there are 16 ounces to the pound, .02835 kilograms per ounce times 16 ounces per pound = 0.45 kilograms per pound.

17. **(C)** ¾ evaporates the second day, therefore there is ¼ of the ⅔ of liquid left after evaporation the first day. ¼ of ⅔ = $^1/_6$, so $^1/_6$ of the original contents remains after two days.

18. **(E)** Compare I and II by finding a common denominator of n(n + 1). I: d (n + 1)/ n(n +

1) = (dn + d)/ n(n + 1). II: (d + 1)n/ n(n + 1) = (dn + n)/ n(n + 1). Since n > d, II > I. Compare I and III. I: d(n − 1)/ n(n − 1) = (dn − d)/ n(n − 1). III: (d − 1)n/ n(n − 1) = (dn − n)/ n(n − 1). Since n > d, dn − d > dn − n, therefore I > III. Compare IV and II. IV: n(n + 1)/ d(n + 1) = n² + n. II: d(d + 1)/ d(n + 1) = d² + d. Since n > d, n² + n > d² + d, so IV > II. Compare V and IV. V: d(n − 1)/ d(d − 1) = (dn − d)/ d(d − 1). IV: (d − 1)n/ d(d − 1) = (dn − n)/ d(d − 1). Since n > d, dn − d > dn − n, so V > IV. Combining what we have found here, III < I < II < IV < V.

19. **(E)** The amount of loss on the article is r% of cost C, or r/100 × C. The selling price is cost minus loss, or S = C − r/100 × C = C(100/ 100 − r/100) = C(100 − r)100.

20. **(B)** Let's start by finding the area of the largest circle. The radius of the largest circle is 9, so the area is 81π. The middle circle has a radius of 5, so the area is 25π. The smallest circle has a radius of 2, so the area is 4π. To find the shaded region we subtract the smaller circle from the middle and get 21π. The fraction is thus $21\pi/81\pi$, which can be lowered to $^7/_{27}$.

21. **(E)** The maximum value is obtained by making X as large as possible and Y as small as possible. Thus, we set up a fraction ½/¾ = ½ × $^4/_3$ = $^4/_6$ = ⅔.

22. **(B)** Let's start by pointing out that we do not know the size of angles 1, 2, 3, or 4. We do know that the two lines are parallel and therefore 8 and 6 can be moved to their corresponding locations on the top line. Since all straight lines have 180 degrees, III and IV equal 180 degrees.

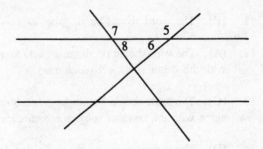

23. **(B)** The square root of .16 is .4, so .16 is a perfect square. The square root of 16 is 4, so 16 is a perfect square. The square root of 1600 is 40, so 1600 is a perfect square. The square root of .0016 is .04, so .0016 is a perfect square. Only 1.6 is not a perfect square.

24. **(A)** By substitution, $x + y^2 - \frac{1}{2}$ becomes $\frac{3}{2} + (2)^2 - \frac{1}{2} = \frac{3}{2} + 4 - \frac{1}{2} = \frac{3}{2} + \frac{8}{2} - \frac{1}{2} = \frac{10}{2} = 5$.

25. **(D)** Solving the equation for x gives x a value of $-\frac{1}{2}$, and $\left| -\frac{1}{2} \right| = \frac{1}{2}$.

Section III

1. **(A)** The singular subject *evidence* requires a singular verb, *suggests*.

2. **(C)** *Carries* must be put into the past (*carried*) to be consistent with the past tense *gathered*.

3. **(B)** Use *who* to refer to persons.

4. **(C)** Change the infinitive to *gathering* so that it is parallel to *manning*.

5. **(A)** The correct word is *uninterested. Disinterested* means "unbiased" or "impartial."

6. **(C)** *It* is redundant and should be omitted.

7. **(E)** This sentence is correct.

8. **(D)** The sentence requires a predicate adjective, *soggy*, to modify the noun *potatoes*.

9. **(B)** The verb required is *blazed*.

10. **(E)** This sentence is correct.

11. **(D)** The word should be singular, *century*.

12. **(A)** The verb should be singular (*has*) to agree with the singular subject (*each one*).

13. **(C)** The verb should be singular (*enables*) to agree with the singular subject *acquaintance*.

14. **(D)** The complement of the infinitive *to be* should be in the objective case (*me*).

15. **(C)** The past tense of the intransitive verb *to lie*, meaning "*to rest or recline*," is *lay*.

16. **(C)** The tense required is the past perfect, *had been drained*.

17. **(E)** This sentence is correct.

18. **(A)** *Irregardless* is nonstandard; use *regardless*.

19. **(B)** A gerund (*joining*) is modified by a possessive pronoun (*his*).

20. **(C)** *Incredulous* means "*unbelieving*"; the word needed is *incredible*, meaning "unbelievable."

21. **(D)** The past tense of the verb *to pass* is *passed*, not *past*.

22. **(D)** The abbreviation *etc.* stands for *et cetera*, meaning *and others*. The use of *and* with *etc.* is therefore redundant.

23. **(E)** This sentence is correct.

24. **(C)** With a compound subject linked by *neither . . . nor*, the verb agrees in number with the closer subject. *Is* should be *are* to agree with *children*.

25. **(E)** This sentence is correct.

26. **(D)** The parts of a compound subject ought to be parallel. *Smoking* is in the same grammatical form as *being*.

27. **(D)** *It's* is the contraction of *it is. Its* is the possessive pronoun.

28. **(E)** A gerund (*going*) is modified by a possessive pronoun (*my*).

29. **(B)** The "if" clause of a past contrary-to-fact condition requires a past perfect subjunctive, always formed with *had*.

30. **(A)** This sentence is correct.

31. **(E)** This sentence combines two ideas: *she never has done any work and she never will do any work*. Do not omit any part of the verb needed to complete the sense.

32. **(C)** *By means of using* is redundant. *Using* conveys the same idea more simply and effectively.

33. **(B)** The dangling phrase makes it sound as if the violence had been interviewed instead of the parents.

34. **(A)** This sentence is correct.

35. **(D)** The awkward and wordy diction of the original is improved by the substitution of a noun phrase in apposition to the subject *Laos*.

36. **(C)** When used as a subject, *everyone* takes a singular verb.

37. **(E)** For the construction to be parallel, *play* needs to be in the same grammatical form as *ski*.

38. **(C)** The two independent clauses should be separated by a semicolon.

39. **(B)** The word *because* is redundant; it performs the same function as the construction *the reason . . . is*.

40. **(D)** In a comparison introduced by *than* or *as*, use the case of the pronoun that you would use if you were completing the comparison. In this instance, the complete form would be *he is as tall as I am tall*; the shortened form is *he is as tall as I am*.

41. **(D)** The verb should be singular (*needs*) to agree with the singular subject *boy*.

42. **(C)** *Walk* should be changed to the past tense, *walked*, to be consistent with the rest of the sentence.

43. **(A)** Use *every one* to refer to every member of a specific group.

44. **(B)** The expression *used to* is found in the past tense only. Do not omit the final *d*.

45. **(E)** This sentence is correct.

46. **(D)** *To emphasize* is needed for parallel structure.

47. **(A)** *Identifying* is not a complete verb; use *identified*.

48. **(A)** *Kind* must be changed to the plural *kinds* to agree with its plural adjective *those* and the plural verb *are*.

49. **(E)** This sentence is correct.

50. **(C)** The correct spelling is *drowned*.

Section IV

1. **(B)** Each tile, including half of the cement around it, has an area of 1 square inch. 3,240 square inches equals 22.5 square feet, or 2.5 square yards.

2. **(D)** $(2 \times 100) + (16 \times 10) + 6 = 200 + 160 + 6 = 366$.

3. **(B)** After the 20% discount, the price was $128. After the 10% discount, the price was $115.20.

4. **(D)** The perimeter of a 46′ × 34′ rectangle is 160 feet, which equals 53⅓ yards.

5. **(E)** After the 15% deduction, $12,750 is left. After the 10% is deducted from $12,750, $11,475 is left. Note that you cannot simply deduct 25% from the $15,000.

6. **(C)** By definition, $(x^a)^b$ is the same as $x^{a \cdot b}$.

7. **(D)** The path of all points equidistant from two points is the perpendicular bisector of the segment which connects the two points. Therefore, the line that is perpendicular to AB and intersects it at 150 miles from A is the perpendicular bisector of AB. (Remember, A and B are 300 miles apart.)

8. **(C)** Substituting r = −3 into Column A, $(-3)^3 + 5(-3)^2 - 6(-3) + 4 = -27 + 45 + 18 + 4 = 40$. Doing the same for Column B,

$3(-3)^2 - 7(-3) - 8 = 27 + 21 - 8 = 40$. Therefore, Columns A and B are equal.

9. **(D)** If $x > 1$ or $-1 < x < 0$, then any number $x > 1/x$. But if $x < -1$ or $0 < x < 1$ then any number $x < 1/x$. Therefore, we cannot tell which column is larger.

10. **(D)** Since we do not know the value of any of the variables, it is impossible to make a determination.

11. **(A)** The angles of triangle ABC are $2m + 3m + 90° = 180°$, $5m = 90°$, $m = 18°$. Angle ACB is $2m = 2 \times 18 = 36°$. Angle ABC is $3m = 3 \times 18 = 54°$. Since angle ABC is the larger angle, the side opposite $\angle$ABC is larger than the side opposite $\angle$ACB. Thus, side AC is larger than side AB.

12. **(A)** Since a ∥ b ∥ c, angle t = angle v, being opposite exterior angles. Therefore, since $\angle u > \angle v$, $\angle u > \angle t$. Also, $\angle s = \angle u$, since they are opposite exterior angles. Therefore, u = s > t. Column A is the larger.

13. **(D)** The circumference of a circle with radius r is $2\pi r$. The area of a circle with radius R is πR^2. If $R > r > \sqrt{2}$, then $\pi R^2 > 2\pi r$. But if $0 < r < R < \sqrt{2}$, then $2\pi r > \pi R^2$. Therefore, we cannot decide which is larger.

14. **(A)** Solving for x in Column A, we can factor $x^2 - 12x + 27 = 0$, $(x - 3)(x - 9) = 0$, so $x = 3,9$. Solving for y in Column B, factor $y^2 + 12y + 27$ so that $(y + 3)(y + 9) = 0$, and $y = -3, -9$. No matter which value of x or y we choose, x is always larger than y, and Column A is larger than Column B.

15. **(B)** In Column A, use long division to solve:

$$\begin{array}{r} n^2 + 3n + 3 \\ n + 2 \overline{)\, n^3 + 5n^2 + 9n + 6} \\ \underline{n^3 + 2n^2} \\ 3n^2 + 9n \\ \underline{3n^2 + 6n} \\ 3n + 6 \\ \underline{3n + 6} \\ 0 \end{array}$$

The fraction $\frac{n^3 + 5n^2 + 9n + 6}{n + 2} = n^2 + 3n + 3$. From Column B, factor a 2 so that $2n^2 + 6n + 6 = 2(n^2 + 3n + 3)$. Thus, Column B is larger than Column A by a factor of 2.

16. **(A)** The easiest way to solve this is to square both sides. Column A becomes 0.9 while column B becomes 0.09.

17. **(D)** If $s > t > 0$, then $s^2 > t^2$. But if $0 > s > t$, then $s^2 < t^2$. We cannot determine which column is the larger.

18. **(A)** a and b are equal so $a + b = 2a = 2(100°) = 200°$. b and d are supplementary angles, so $b + d = 180°$. Column A is larger than Column B.

19. **(B)** In Column B, a = b = c, so $b + c = 100° + 100° = 200°$, which is more than Column A's value of 180°.

20. **(C)** Since a and d are supplementary angles, $d = 180° - a$.

21. **(A)** $(½)x - (½)a = 4$. Multiplying both sides of the equation by 2, $x - a = 8$, and $x = 8 + a$. Adding 8 to any real number will make it larger; therefore, x is the larger number.

22. **(B)** The values of Column A and Column B are 12 and 21, respectively. Therefore, Column B is the larger.

23. **(D)** Since side AB = side AC, △ABC is isosceles, and it can be assumed that $\angle$B and $\angle$C are equal. This information, though, does not provide any clues as to which is bigger, $\angle$A or $\angle$B.

24. **(A)** It is obvious that the length of AB is 6. The length of CD is $\sqrt{[3-(-2)]^2 + (4-3)^2} = \sqrt{26}$, or approximately 5.10. Therefore, AB is longer.

25. **(D)** Vertical angles are equal in degree, but this does not divulge the information needed to determine which column is larger.

26. **(A)** The values of Column A and Column B

are 4¹/₁₆ and 2¼, respectively. Therefore, Column A is larger than Column B.

27. **(D)** The value of Column A is $2xy^2$. Since it is not known whether y is positive or negative, it cannot be determined which column is larger.

28. **(C)** If x is the original cost of one radio, to sell at a 25% loss means x − .25x = $120, or .75x = $120. Thus, the original cost was $160. The loss was $160 − $120 = $40. If y is the original cost of the second radio sold at a 25% gain, y + .25y = $120 or 1.25y = $120. The original price was $96. The gain was $120 − $96 = $24. The total loss was $40 − $24 = $16.

29. **(E)** The difference between the numbers increases by 2; therefore, ? − 20 = 10, so ? = 30.

30. **(D)** The area of the square is 36. Since the triangle is equilateral, we can use the 30 : 60 : 90 rule to solve. By dropping a perpendicular we can figure out the altitude to be $3\sqrt{3}$. Then the area of the triangle is $9\sqrt{3}$.

31. **(A)** ²/₅ = .4. $\sqrt{.4}$ is closest to .6 since $(.6)^2$ = .36.

32. **(D)** Drawing a line from the top perpendicular to the bottom, we create a rectangle with two right triangles:

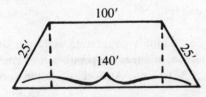

The base of each right triangle is ½(140 − 100) = 20′. The height of each is $\sqrt{25^2 - 20^2}$ = $\sqrt{225}$ = 15′. The area of each right triangle is ½(20) (15) = 150 sq. ft. The area of the rectangle is (15)(100) = 1,500 sq. ft. The total area of the dam is 150 + 150 + 1500 = 1,800 sq. ft.

33. **(E)** Multiplying the equation by t,
$$t\left(1 + \frac{1}{t}\right) = t\left(\frac{t+1}{t}\right); \text{ becomes } t + 1 = t + 1.$$

t can be any real number; therefore, a single value of t cannot be determined.

34. **(E)** Draw a circle with point A at its center and a radius of 6 inches. All points on the circle will be 6 inches from A. Draw two lines, one one inch above line b and the other one inch below line b.

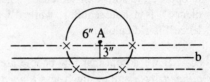

Where the circle and lines intersect are the points both 6 inches from point A and 1 inch from line b.

35. **(E)** Let R = 5 and S = 10, both being integers divisible by 5. But R + S = 5 + 10 = 15, which is not divisible by 10.

Section V

1. **(E)** Someone who is *obstinate* "unreasonably clings to a particular persuasion or point of view" and hence is unlikely to *cooperate*.

2. **(B)** *Rancor* is "strong ill will toward something," whereas *affection* is "fondness for something."

3. **(B)** What is *capricious* is "erratic," whereas what is *stable* is "firm or secure."

4. **(D)** What is *cryptic* "obscures," whereas what is *revealing* "discloses."

5. **(D)** *Perseverance* is a "condition of persisting," whereas *cessation* is an "ending."

6. **(C)** Something *saturated* is "completely filled with something," whereas something *barren* is "desolate" or "empty."

7. **(B)** Something *atrocious* is "horrible," whereas something *excellent* is "extremely good."

8. **(B)** Something *intelligible* "can be comprehended," whereas something *unclear* is "difficult to comprehend."

9. **(E)** To *uproot* is to "displace," whereas to *insert* is to "put or place in."

10. **(E)** *Animosity* is "hostility toward someone," whereas *friendliness* is "good will toward someone."

11. **(D)** A council of ministers would be expected to oppose the spread of violence. "*Sensible* violence" is a non sequitur, while "*senile* violence" is ridiculous.

12. **(E)** If we accept that few people are actually *blinded* by a smile, much less *tanned* by one, we see that (E) best completes the thought.

13. **(D)** A miser cannot be a *spendthrift*, or loose with money, while gifts to charity are never *tasteless* or *selfish*.

14. **(B)** To disarm someone in a single motion requires sure and swift, or *deft*, action.

15. **(C)** A publication appearing twice a month would be a *semimonthly* ("half"-monthly) publication. To say "a *periodical* magazine" is redundant.

16. **(D)** A *teacher* gives *instruction*, and a *watchman* gives *protection*.

17. **(A)** One is received at a *restaurant* by a *hostess* and at an *office* by a *receptionist*.

18. **(C)** One *skates* on a *rink* and *reposes* on a *bed*.

19. **(C)** A *sapling* is a young *tree*, and a *puppy* is a young *dog*.

20. **(C)** To *fret* is necessarily not to *relax*, and to *fight* is necessarily not to *submit*.

21. **(B)** If we *stutter*, our *talking* is impeded. If we *stumble*, our *walking* is impeded.

22. **(A)** To *destroy* is to *demolish*, and to *cry* is to *wail*.

23. **(E)** Both a *chimney* and a *funnel* are greater in dimensions at one end than at the other. The former is used to transfer *fumes*, and the latter to transfer *liquid*.

24. **(B)** The *characteristic* of something is relevant to its *quality*, and the *volume* of something is relevant to its *quantity*.

25. **(C)** A *conductor* leads his *orchestra*, and a *coach* leads his *team*.

26. **(A)** The first sentence of the selection as well as its reference to Hong King's partnership with British administration and enterprise supports answer (A) as the correct response to this question. Answer (B) is not correct, as the Chinese refugees were an asset, not a hindrance, to Hong Kong's financial status. There is no reference in the passage to African nations; therefore, answer (C) is wrong. Choice (D) is inaccurate because the British acquired Hong Kong by treaty, not by military force. Hong Kong, with its great population, does not lack skilled workers; thus, choice (E) is also wrong.

27. **(E)** With the Korean War came Hong Kong's most dramatic economic change—a switch in concentration from trading to manufacturing. Thus, answer (E) is the correct response.

28. **(B)** Choice (A) cannot be supported. Responses (C) and (D) had positive effects upon Hong Kong's trade and therefore cannot be considered correct answers. Answer (E) is wrong, because this change did not take place. The article's reference to Hong Kong's continuing prosperity until it fell to the Japanese supports answer (B) as the right response to the question.

29. **(C)** China's population is larger than 700 million, whereas the population of Hong Kong is 3¾ million. Answer (C) is the correct answer.

30. **(C)** Since Hong Kong exports 90% of its products and the U.S. imports about 25% of them, this leaves 65% for all other nations; therefore, answer (A) is inaccurate. Answer (B) is not correct, because some of its exports are partly (not exclusively) made in Hong Kong. Answer (D) is not correct, because the article states that 40% (not 50%) of Hong Kong's labor force is engaged in manufacturing. Answer (E) is a false statement, because at one point the U.N. placed an embargo on Hong Kong's ex-

ports. Answer (C) is the correct response because the article states that Malaysia, Canada, and West Germany are excellent markets for Hong Kong's products.

31. **(B)** Statements (A) and (C) are much too general to be indicative of the article's purpose. Answer (D) is not correct because the dangers of neutrinos are not discussed. Answer (E), although mentioned, was not the purpose of the article. The selection as a whole describes the search for neutrinos, so choice (B) is the correct answer.

32. **(D)** The existence of neutrinos is based purely on theory. Neutrinos have not yet been found or observed. Paragraph two discusses this in detail. Answers (A), (B), (C), and (E) are all incorrect responses. The right answer is (D).

33. **(A)** The neutrino is described as a particle having a vanishingly small mass; because of this, it can be detected only inferentially. Answer (A) is the correct response. Since a neutrino has never been observed, a comparison in size to anything else would be inaccurate, making choices (B), (C), and (E) wrong. (D) is also wrong because neutrinos have not been observed.

34. **(D)** Answer (A) is an incorrect response, as there is no information in the passage to support this conclusion. (B) is wrong because scientists are still working to prove the existence of neutrinos. Choices (C) and (E) are also incorrect answers since there has been no validated observation of the neutrino. The correct answer is choice (D), which is supported by the author's statement that the neutrino theory is an integral part of physics.

35. **(B)** The correct choice is (B). According to the final paragraph, "Certain quantities that physicists insist should be the same after an interaction as before . . . could only be con-

served if another particle of zero charge and negligible mass were emitted." As the neutrino cannot be observed, choice (E) is incorrect, and no plausible mention of magnetism, inertia, or motion is made.

36. **(C)** The author of this article is not criticizing our institutions. He is, in fact, saying that we must not destroy institutions but should search for change by peaceful means. Considering that, answers (B), (D), and (E) are inaccurate responses to the question. The writer does offer certain suggestions for change, but more importantly he urges these forces of change through moderation, condemning violence, destruction, and rage as a means of achieving these changes. Choice (C) is the best answer.

37. **(D)** Paragraph eight states that "the fight for a better world is a long one." Answer (D) is the correct response. Answers (A), (B), (C), and (E) are all wrong choices as they do not support the author's thesis.

38. **(C)** Paragraph seven of the passage discusses violence as a result of authoritarians, which can be interpreted to mean politicians. Answer (C) is thus the correct choice. The same paragraph also states that a better society is not built by violence, so choice (D) is wrong. Answer (B) is also wrong because dynamism is an element of dissent, so it would not contribute to itself. Answers (A) and (E) play no part in the discussion and are incorrect.

39. **(D)** The last paragraph of the selection outlines the qualities of a good public official. All answer choices except education (answer D) are mentioned. (D), then, is the correct choice.

40. **(D)** "The anarchist plays into the hands of the authoritarian." This sentence from paragraph seven supports answer (D) as the correct response. All other responses are false statements.

SUGGESTIONS FOR FURTHER READING

We would like to recommend several related Arco titles that will be of particular interest to readers of this book:

Books Relating to the Military

OFFICER CANDIDATE TESTS by Solomon Wiener, Colonel AUS. (Ret.). Here is both an overview of military testing and specific information about each of the officer selection tests including the Air Force Officer Qualifying Test (AFOQT), the Army Officer Selection Battery (OSB) and Flight Officer Selection Tests (FAST), and the Navy and Marine Corps Aviation Selection Battery. Over 2400 questions divided among 28 skill areas offer officer candidates practice with every subject on which they will be tested.

YOU AND THE ARMED FORCES by Texe Marrs. Military life is thoroughly examined with information on career specialities and education training programs, sources of officer appointment, salaries and benefits for enlistees and officers, and the special requirements.

Books to Prepare for the SAT and the ACT

PREPARATION FOR THE SAT (SCHOLASTIC APTITUDE TEST) by Brigitte Saunders et al. Six full-length practice exams with detailed explanatory answers to all questions. Expert review material for both verbal and mathematics sections of the exam.

VERBAL WORKBOOK FOR THE SAT by Elizabeth Morse-Cluley, Walter James Miller, Gabriel P. Freedman and Margaret A. Haller. Comprehensive review for the verbal and TSWE sections of the SAT. Hundreds of graded practice questions for review in each area. Five full-length practice tests with explanatory answers. Progress charts for self-evaluation.

MATHEMATICS WORKBOOK FOR THE SAT by Brigitte Saunders with David Frieder and Mark Weinfeld. Authoritative instructional text and extensive drill in all math areas covered on the SAT. Diagnostic tests in each area to spotlight weaknesses; post-tests to measure progress. Three sample tests with complete solutions.

VOCABULARY BUILDER FOR THE SAT by Edward J. Deptula et al. This is the ideal publication to test vocabulary skills in preparing for the examination. Both entertaining and challenging, this text offers students a new way to increase their vocabulary skills.

AMERICAN COLLEGE TESTING PROGRAM (ACT) by Eve P. Steinberg. Four full-length practice test batteries with explanatory answers for all questions. Skills reviews and practice questions in each subject area of the exam. Detailed directions for scoring and evaluating exam results. Valuable test-taking tips.

VERBAL WORKBOOK FOR THE ACT by Joyce Lakritz. Intensive review for the English Usage and Reading Comprehension sections of the ACT. Three full-length sample ACT English Usage Tests with explanatory answers to help candidates assess their readiness for the ACT.

MATHEMATICS WORKBOOK FOR THE ACT by Barbara Erdsneker and Brigitte Saunders. In-depth review of the mathematical concepts essential to scoring high on the ACT. Diagnostic tests in each area, followed by instructional text and practice problems, with re-tests to measure progress. Three sample ACT Mathematics Tests with detailed solutions.